THE WILDLIFE COMPANION

Edited by Malcolm Tait
and Olive Tayler

Ex Libris

Chris Buckingham
Sharpenhoe
#44 1582 882973

A THINK BOOK FOR

ROBSON BOOKS

The Cook's Companion
Edited by Jo Swinnerton
ISBN 1-86105-772-5

The Gardener's Companion
Edited by Vicky Bamforth
ISBN 1-86105-771-7

The Traveller's Companion
Edited by Georgina Newbery and Rhiannon Guy
ISBN 1-86105-773-3

SERIES EDITORS

Malcolm Tait and Emma Jones

If one really loves nature,
one can find beauty everywhere.

Vincent van Gogh

T H I N K
A Think Book
for Robson Books

First published in Great Britain in 2004 by
Robson Books
The Chrysalis Building, Bramley Road, London W10 6SP

An imprint of **Chrysalis** Books Group plc

Edited by Malcolm Tait and Olive Tayler
The Companion team: Vicky Bamforth, Sarah Bove, James Collins,
Harry Glass, Rhiannon Guy, Annabel Holmes, Emma Jones
and Lou Millward Tait

Think Publishing
The Pall Mall Deposit
124-128 Barlby Road, London W10 6BL
www.thinkpublishing.co.uk

The Wildlife Trusts' UK Office
The Kiln, Waterside, Mather Road, Newark, Nottinghamshire NG24 1WT
www.wildlifetrusts.org

ISBN 1-86105-770-9

Printed and bound by Clays Ltd, Bungay, Suffolk NR35 1ED

Nature does nothing uselessly.

Aristotle

PLEASE GO WILD FOR THE FOLLOWING...

This book would not have been possible without the
research, ideas, and dogged support of:

Claire Ashton, Deb Bright, Rachel Cullen,
Tim and Paulette Doncaster, Katherine Lawrey,
James Marshall, Audrey McAuliffe, Nigel Millward,
Peter Tait and Geordie Torr.

If you think you're buying a worthy reference book, think again. But if you're looking for an original and humorous snapshot of the natural world, look no further. *The Wildlife Companion* opens up vistas that will amuse and inform the most learned experts on nature and conservation.

Yet the secret of this miscellany is its alternative take on wildlife which is certain to have a broad appeal. Even those who would normally shun the animal and plant kingdom cannot fail to be captivated by the wry observations, charming descriptions and torrent of fascinating nature 'trivia'.

This encyclopaedic material is not just natural fodder for the pub quiz night, it will nourish the minds of anyone curious and hungry for knowledge, young and old. The information may have a greater resonance for devotees of the country walk, connoiseurs of safaris and expeditions to the outback. But this canter through the undergrowth and by-ways of our environment cannot fail to raise a smile and strengthen respect for the living world.

This guide will teach you to mind your Jills and Kittens, Hoglets and Scats. It will introduce you to a Cawdy Mawdy, a Mouldiwarp, Hornywink, Leopard's bane and Fiddle dock. So much enthusiasm is whipped up in this little book, membership of Wildlife Trusts and conservation groups should flourish.

The armchair adventurer may even be inspired to discover the real outdoors.

Valerie Elliott, The Times Countryside Editor

THE FOOTIE FALCON

Soon after the second world war, a games enthusiast called Peter Adolph put together a few tabletop figures and invented a game that was to capture the hearts (and fingers) of small boys everywhere. But he had a problem. He wanted to protect the name of the game – Hobby – but found that he was unable to gain copyright for a word in such common usage. It was the bird world that came to his rescue. He discovered that there is a small falcon called a hobby, so named the game after the bird's Latin name.

The hobby's generic name is *Falco*, but its specific name comes from the fact that it was once seen as a sub-class of buzzard, the Latin name for which is *Buteo*. Thus it was that the hobby, the Subbuteo, lent its name to the most enduring tabletop football game of all time.

7 SPECIES THAT AREN'T WHAT THEY SAY THEY ARE

Little mouse-ear is actually a plant
Wood hedgehog is actually a fungus
Garden tiger is actually a moth
Yellow bird's-nest is actually a plant
Brilliant emerald is actually a dragonfly
Fat hen is actually a plant
Ragged robin is actually a plant
Incidentally, ragged robin is not named after the bird, but the folklore elf Robin Goodfellow, who appeared as Puck in Shakespeare's A Midsummer's Night's Dream

SITES FOR SORE EYES

One of the most spectacular geological sites in the country is Earl's Hill in Shropshire. Its main hill, when viewed from one angle, looks like a sleeping dragon, which is particularly appropriate as it was created by fiery layers of lava that burst from the rocks 650 million years ago. In more recent times, an iron age hill fort was built on its summit in around 600 BC.

Today, Earl's Hill is a magnificent nature reserve. Its woods of hazel, ash, oak, field maple, holly and yew are awash with bluebells, while dippers and grey wagtails can be spotted flying just along the stream, or bobbing up and down on rocks. The old meadowland contains yellow meadow anthills, while over 30 species of butterfly have been recorded here. In 1964 it became the first reserve to be launched by the Shropshire Wildlife Trust.

NATURE NOTES

Now I don't usually hug trees, but on the evening of 5 January 1991 I made an exception. For three days the weatherman on Irish television had been tracking an interesting hole in the Atlantic pressure system; he forecast, rather too cheerfully I thought, that a severe storm would hit Ireland early in the morning of 6 January. I went out in the evening of the 5th and stood contemplating the old beeches in the garden: 19 of them. I guessed they were a little under 200 years old and 100ft high. Why had I not looked at them more carefully before? The evening was absolutely still with the patch of red in the western sky that is supposed to delight shepherds. Pessimistically I put my faith in the weatherman. I slipped a tape measure round the smooth, silver-green, lichen-encrusted bellies of the trees and listed the measurements in a notebook. None was a record breaker. But all had been good friends to five generations of our family. As I taped each tree, I gave it a hug, as if to say 'good luck tonight'.

Thomas Pakenham, *Meetings with Remarkable Trees*
By the time the storm was over, only seven of the 19 beeches still stood

FROGS ARE FUNNY

A lonely frog goes to a fortune-teller to find out his future. The fortune-teller gazes deep into her crystal ball and peers through its mists. Finally, she looks up. 'You are going to meet a beautiful young girl who will want to know everything about you.' The frog is thrilled. 'This is brilliant! Where will I meet her? At work? At a party?' 'No' says the fortune-teller, 'at a biology class.'

NOSTALGIC NONSENSE

Readers from the black and white TV generation may remember a children's programme called *Tales of the Riverbank*, in which, *Wind in the Willows* style, three rodent friends carried out their adventures alongside an idyllic flowing river. The programme was narrated by Johnny Morris, and children didn't seem to care that Roddy the white rat, Hammy the hamster and Gordon the guinea pig weren't British anyway.

But then neither was the riverbank itself. The series was shot between 1959 and 1961 in Toronto, although a 1970s follow-up, called *Hammy the Hamster*, was filmed in the Isle of Wight. At the end of filming of the latter, some of the animals escaped, and rumours persist that a colony of guinea pigs made part of the island their own for many years afterwards... perhaps still surviving there to this very day?

Identifying animals from their tracks, or spoor, is easier than you might think. The best place to look for animal tracks is on soft ground so if it hasn't rained recently, try looking close to a river or stream where the mud is soft, whatever the weather. Tracks are particularly noticeable after snowfall, and where the earth is clear of human or pet footprints. However, do not stray off established paths in your investigative enthusiasm – you never know what you might crush or scare off as you stride through the undergrowth. Stick to the paths, keep an eye on the mud and Happy Tracking!

BADGER

Broad with five digits and a large kidney-shaped pad

FOX

Narrow and tear shaped, four digits

OTTER

Five digit tracks with an almost round pad

DEER

Cloven hooved

RABBIT

Four digits, poorly defined due to fur

SQUIRREL

Four digits on front foot, five digits on rear foot

RATS OR MICE

Similar to squirrel but with wider spread digits at rear

CAT

Very rounded tracks with four digits, claws rarely visible

DOG

Broad ovals with four digits. Claws often visible

PIRATE

Often an erratic track to follow

Nature hides have a code of their own, which can make them quite intimidating to the newcomer. Here are six tips to help you avoid looking like a wildlife virgin:

1. Don't stick your arm out of the window while you're pointing at that pretty little duck

The reason that hides exist is to fool the wildlife into thinking that they're alone in their environment. Waving arms and pointing fingers can destroy the illusion, as well as your own credibility. Leaving the door open once you've gone in can do the same.

2. Keep quiet

Sotto voce is a good motto – this isn't a zoo, after all. Not only might your raised voice disturb the wildlife, it can also be an irritating interruption to the gentle contemplation of nature being enjoyed by the other occupants of the hide. Keep your voice down as you approach the hide, too.

3. Don't pretend to be David

While you're sitting there watching the birds and animals, and surrounded by whispering adults, you must resist the temptation to do a David Attenborough. The urge wears off after about your third or fourth visit, so if you do break into a breathless: 'And out here, just in front of me, one of nature's most enigmatic creatures is about to perform a dance rarely seen by the human eye', then you've given yourself away.

4. Don't clutter the place up

Leaving your rucksack, thermos flask, ID books and bag of goodies from the gift shop strewn on the seats means that you might be stopping someone else from enjoying the view. In addition, that space between the benches is not a handy storage area for carrier bags, it's a viewing point for wheelchair users.

5. Don't worry about not knowing

Although the camouflaged, equipment-carrying, wisely-nodding hordes around you may look as if they'd frown upon the ignorant, if you really have no idea what that little brown job is that's wandering around right in front of you, then don't be afraid to ask. Most nature lovers are delighted to be able to share their knowledge, and you'll probably find out even more about what you're watching than a guidebook could tell you.

6. Stay there

If you've got the time, give it at least 30 minutes. You may feel that you've seen everything from a particular hide within the first five minutes, but part of the great pleasure is the wait for the unexpected appearance, or the sudden change in behaviour. A hobby flashing past as it grabs a dragonfly; a heron quickly stabbing at an eel, the seemingly new view as the light changes across a lake: these and many more delights are only seen by the patient.

If ever proof was wanted that our hearts lie in the countryside, then we can find it in the way we name our homes. Of the 50 leading house names in Britain, according to a recent survey, all bar a handful are based on rural hankerings:

1. The Cottage	26. Woodside
2. Rose Cottage	27. Meadow View
3. The Bungalow	28. The Stables
4. The Coach House	29. The White House
5. Orchard House	30. Holly Cottage
6. The Lodge	31. Willow Cottage
7. Woodlands	32. Highfield
8. The Old School House	33. The Haven
9. Ivy Cottage	34. Springfield
10. The Willows	35. Fairview
11. The Barn	36. White Cottage
12. The Old Rectory	37. Mill House
13. Hillside	38 The Orchard
14. Hillcrest	39. Treetops
15. The Croft	40. Primrose Cottage
16. The Old Vicarage	41. The Granary
17. Sunnyside	42. The Nook
18. Orchard Cottage	43. Corner Cottage
19. Yew Tree Cottage	44. School House
20. The Laurels	45. Greenacres
21. The Old Post Office	46. The Old School
22. The Gables	47. Honeysuckle Cottage
23. The Hollies	48. Lilac Cottage
24. The Beeches	49. Wayside
25. The Firs	50. Oaklands

Although no animals appear in the top 50, not far outside this list come Badgers Cottage, Cuckoo Cottage, Curlew Cottage, Dolphin Cottage, Fox Hollow, Kestrels, Magpies, Mole End, Nightingale Cottage, Robin Hill, Rookery Nook, Squirrels Leap, Swallow Barn, The Jays and Two Hoots.

CRYPTIC CREATURES AND PUZZLING PLANTS

My first is in badger and also in bird
My second's in seen and also in heard
My third is in petal and stamen and leaf
My fourth is in common but never in heath
My fifth is in hornet but never in bee
My whole is a tree that sounds good by the sea
Answer on page 153

NATURE NOTES

Many people, even 'lovers of Nature', would be inclined to look for small beer in a book with the title of *Adventures among Birds*. If they are ignorant of Mr [WH] Hudson's writings, they are not to blame, since bird books are, as a rule, small beer. Most writers condescend to birds or have not the genius to keep them alive in print, whether or not they have the eternal desire 'to convey to others', as Mr Hudson says, 'some faint sense or suggestion of the wonder and delight which may be found in Nature'. He does not condescend to birds, 'these loveliest of our fellow-beings,' as he calls them, 'these which give greatest beauty and lustre to the world'. He travels 'from county to county viewing many towns and villages, conversing with persons of all ages and conditions,' and when these persons are his theme he writes like a master, like an old master perhaps, as everybody knows who has read his *Green Mansions*, *The Purple Land*, and *South American Sketches*. It might, therefore, be taken for granted that such an artist would not be likely to handle birds unless he could do so with the same reality and vitality as men. And this is what he does.

Edward Thomas, *In Pursuit of Spring,* 1914

THE WEASEL IS WEASELLY RECOGNISED BUT THE STOAT IS STOATALLY DIFFERENT

If only that were the case. Stoats and weasels, as they flash by in hot pursuit of a leveret or rodent, are very hard to tell apart in the wild. Often all you're left with is an image of a brown and white, elongated creature with its legs stretched out before and behind like a tiny cheetah.

The stoat, however, is much bigger than the weasel, on average weighing three times more. Should you catch sight of the tail, a long tail with a black-furred tip will give away the stoat's presence. The weasel's tail is shorter without the black. Along the body, there is a clearly defined line between the brown and white on a stoat, whereas the two colours blur more in the middle on a weasel.

If you see the animal in winter, life gets easier. Stoats grow white coats – ermine – during the cold months, whereas weasels maintain their summer garb.

QUOTE UNQUOTE

Man is the only creature that consumes without producing.
GEORGE ORWELL, novelist and essayist

ON GOSSAMER WINGS

Gossamer is name given to the light, filmy money spider webs that appear in grasses on sunny autumn mornings. The name comes from a contraction of goose summer, ie St Martin's summer, the feast day in November when geese were once traditionally eaten. The tiny spiders are able to spin their webs across such great distances by allowing themselves to be wafted along on autumn breezes as they spin.

10 SURE SIGNS THAT YOU'RE A WEREWOLF

1. You wake up naked in a field a couple of times a month
2. You have an unusually passionate hatred of vegetarians except with mayonnaise
3. Your friends call you Hairy McLairy
4. You have an above average tendency to bite your tongue
5. You can trace your family tree back to Lon Chaney Jr
6. Your nose-hair clippers keep breaking
7. Moonlight becomes you, it goes with your hair
8. A shop has recently opened down the high street selling silver bullets
9. Your other friends call you Wolfgang de Wolf, or Wolfie for short
10. You keep finding yourself wondering if Mowgli's doing OK

A WHEEL GOOD TIME

Dragonflies have evolved a complex and sometimes time-consuming position for mating, called the wheel. This is a unique approach in animal mating, because it uses the fact that male dragonflies have secondary genital equipment.

The primary genitals in both genders are in the latter segments of their abdomens, ie at the far end of the body. Yet prior to copulation, the male is able to transfer his sperm up the length of his abdomen towards his main torso. He then clasps the female's head with the end of his abdomen, using pincers that are shaped to fit grooves along the side of her head, and if his enticement is successful, she bends her abdomen upwards until the tip of it, where her genitals lie, are in contact with the upper part of his own abdomen, where his sperm now lies; the wheel is formed, and the fun begins.

And what fun it is. Although in some species, copulation can last for just a few seconds, in others the process can last hours, sometimes up to six. It's a fascinating event to watch, but beware: after a few minutes you do begin to feel like a bit of a voyeur.

I think that I shall never see
A billboard lovely as a tree
Perhaps unless the billboards fall
I'll never see a tree at all.
OGDEN NASH, US humorist

WILD ABOUT WILDLIFE

When Shakespeare gave Hotspur the line 'Nay, I'll have a starling shall be taught to speak nothing' in *Henry IV Part 1* he would have had no idea what this allusion was to bring about.

Eugene Scheiffelin was a 19th century American Shakespeare fanatic with an equally crazy love of wildlife, who found a way to combine his two loves: release each of the 55 species of bird mentioned in Shakespeare into America. He had no real success, except with the starlings. Scheiffelin released 60 of the birds into New York City's Central Park in 1890, and 40 more the following year, and by 1950 the population had risen to many millions, the birds even reaching the Pacific Ocean. By the 1960s California, for example, decided to cull the starlings because they had become such a pest. Over nine million birds were slaughtered, but it proved impossible to kill every starling in the state, and numbers soon built back up again.

Today, there are approximately 200 million European starlings in America, a full third of the world's population.

BY NAME, BY NATION

There are various practices for naming new dinosaur finds, one of the commonest being the place in which you found it. To date, there has been no record of a Grimsbychus or a Sloughraptor, and we can only hope that there might one day be a Llanfairpwllgwyngyllgogerych-wyrndrobwyll-llantysiliogogogochosaurus, but in the meantime, the following will have to do:

Albertosaurus .... Alberta, Canada
Andesaurus .... The Andes mountains, South America
Coloradisaurus .... Colorado Formation in Argentina
Denversaurus .... Denver, Colorado, USA
Edmontosaurus .... Edmonton Formation in Alberta, Canada
Indosaurus and Indosuchus .... India
Lesothosaurus .... Lesotho, southern Africa
Utahraptor .... Utah, USA
Szechuanosaurus .... Szechuan, China

Of all the patron saints, perhaps the most famous is the one designated to the animals, St Francis of Assisi.

Francis Bernardone was born at Assisi in Umbria in 1181 or 1182. His father was a successful merchant, and Francis dreamed either of emulating him, or of becoming a noble knight. While following the latter path, he took part in an attack on Perugia at the age of 20, but was captured and imprisoned for a year, during which time he turned to religion.

By his mid-20s, he was devoting himself to the Church, much to his father's shame. Now it was the turn of his father to imprison him, but he did not give up his faith, going on to found a brotherhood on behalf of Pope Innocent III known as the Friars Minor. They would later become the Franciscans. With his order he travelled Italy preaching and emphasising the importance of simplicity and poverty. He was joined in 1212 by Clara Sciffi, a rich girl from Assisi who was so taken by his cause that she founded her own sisterhood, the Poor Clares.

Finding the management of men too disruptive, Francis eventually went to the mountains to live among the animals in seclusion and prayer. He died in 1226, and his feast day is October 4.

Not all patron saints had such love of animals, however. St Hubert was a son of the 7th century Duke of Aquitaine who loved the chase. One Good Friday, while out hunting a deer, he was amazed to find the stag turning to him, with a cross between its antlers, stating: 'Hubert, unless you turn to the Lord, and lead a holy life, you shall quickly fall into the abyss of Hell!' Hubert did as he was bid, distributed his wealth and turned to the Church. He died some years later while reciting the Lord's Prayer, and with a somewhat cruel irony, having renounced his early destructive days, was given November 3 as a feast day, and the title patron saint of hunters. Incidentally, if your profession is smelter or maker of precision instruments, then he's your patron saint too.

St Patrick, patron saint of Ireland, deserves a mention too, as he was believed to have given a hilltop sermon that rid the country of snakes. There are some who argue that they could have done that, too, seeing as Ireland never had any snakes in the first place, but who's quibbling.

CRYPTIC CREATURES AND PUZZLING PLANTS

Unravel the following:
GANIGHTLE
Answer on page 153

STRANGELY OMITTED FROM THE I-SPY BOOK OF ANIMALS

Catoblepas (also known as gorgon – not to be confused with its namesake that has a head full of snakes). Admire from distance. If mane rises, flee with reasonable speed, as catoblepas is about to emit noxious fumes that will leave you writhing in fatal convulsions. Makes poor pet. Score: 40 pts.

FROGS ARE FUNNY

A frog goes into a job centre, hops up to the counter and asks 'Got a job?'

The man behind the counter looks around for a moment, then notices the frog down below. 'I beg your pardon', he says. 'Did you say something?' 'Sure did,' says the frog. 'Wondered if you've got anything going?' The man is beside himself. A talking frog! 'Look, why don't you come back tomorrow. I'm sure I'll have something for you then.'

The frog leaves, and the man is on the phone immediately, phoning the circus, the TV chat shows, the newspapers and anyone else he can think of who'll pay handsomely for this scoop.

The next day the frog comes back. 'So, got a job?' he asks.

'You bet', says the man, rubbing his hands. 'I've lined you up with an exclusive with the *Daily Mail*, your own TV series, and a long-running job in the circus. I'll just take the customary 10%. What do you think about that?'

'Chat shows? The circus?' frowns the frog. 'That's no good. I'm a welder.'

Cley, on the north Norfolk coast, is a birdwatcher's heaven. Its fresh and saltwater marshes provide feeding, roosting and breeding opportunities for a host of species, while the surrounding area contains habitats as diverse as shingle and dune, mudflats, ancient heathland and deciduous woodland, as well as magnificent vantage points for excellent sea-watching.

The east bank of the reserve is thought by many to be the best birding spot in the country. Not only does it give fine views of wildfowl and wading flocks, but the adjacent pools are frequently host to any number of unusual and passage species. One of the best nature-watchers to recognise its value was the one-time Cley warden and birding legend Richard Richardson, who could frequently be found in the 1940s, 1950s, 1960s and 1970s standing on its muddy path, watching and sketching the birds below and above, and who, as writer Richard Mabey once said, 'had the uncanny knack of being able to see the world from a bird's point of view'.

Cley was The Wildlife Trusts very first reserve, purchased by the then fledgeling Norfolk Naturalists' Trust in 1926.

QUOTE UNQUOTE

Humans are the only animals that have children on purpose – with the exception of guppies, who like to eat theirs.
PJ O'ROURKE, travel writer

DON'T BE KOI

Herons are not exactly on the Christmas card list of the nation's ornamental fish owners, their predilection for shiny, easily catchable pond fare driving many a suburban gardener to distraction. Yet there's one Northampton family whose prize koi had a lucky and quite bizarre escape from the hungry bird.

Sitting around their glowing winter fireplace, they glanced out of the window, and noticed the heron pluck one of their wriggling koi from the pond at the end of the garden. In a panic, they yelled and waved their arms, but too late... the bird had taken wing and the fish was gone.

But not for long. Perhaps startled by the frantic family, perhaps unused to the size of the fish, the heron was unable to hold onto it. As it flew over the house, it dropped it... straight down the chimney onto the hot coals in the grate, from where it bounced onto the living room carpet. The heron went hungry, and the fish, little more than scratched, survived.

NATURE NOTES

I love Nature partly because she is not man, but a retreat from him.
None of his institutions control or pervade her. There a different kind
of right prevails. In her midst I can be glad with an entire gladness. If
this world were all man, I could not stretch myself, I should lose all
hope. He is constraint, she is freedom to me. He makes me wish for
another world. She makes me content with this.

Henry David Thoreau, *A Writer's Journal*

7 GREAT SCRABBLE NAMES

Ouabaio ....an African tree, good for using up vowels
Zyxmyia...a type of fly
Pnyxia ....another type of fly
Xyzzors..a nemotode. Oh, for another 'z'
O-O ....a bird
Coccaceae ....bacteria. Clean up on your 'c's
Dixid ....yet another fly

GREAT SCOTT

*I had looked forward to helping you to bring him up, but it is a
satisfaction to know that he will be safe with you... Make the boy
interested in natural history if you can. It is better than games.*

These were among Captain Robert Falcon Scott's last written words to
his wife Kathleen as he lay dying in a tent in an Antarctic blizzard in
1912. He was referring to his two-year-old son Peter, (named after
Peter Pan, the creation of his godfather, JM Barrie), who was born on
13 September 1909, the very day that Scott announced his plans to
travel south.

Peter did indeed become interested in natural history. Very
interested. He became one of the leading conservationists of the 20th
century, and the first to be knighted for his work.

Dubbed 'the father of conservation' by David Bellamy, and
conservation's 'patron saint' by David Attenborough, Scott founded
the Wildfowl & Wetlands Trust, was first chairman of the World
Wildlife Fund (now the Worldwide Fund for Nature), originator of the
World Conservation Union Red Data Books, and founder of many
regional conservation bodies from the Gloucestershire Trust for Nature
Conservation to the Falkland Islands Foundation (later Falkland
Conservation). He was a prolific wildlife artist, saviour of the
Hawaiian goose, and championship level dinghy racer and skater for
good measure. In short, interested in natural history AND games.

Florence Nightingale, nurse extraordinaire, had a great love of birds. 'There is nothing makes my heart thrill like the voice of birds, much more than the human voice. It is the angels calling us with their songs.' Living in London near the gardens of the Dorchester Hotel, she would happily feed the birds, watching and listening to them: 'There is a thrush here. We fed him during the winter – he is so good as to sing in the trees opposite my bedroom windows, in all the din of Park Lane, the only thrush I ever heard sing in London.' To her childhood home, she wrote asking for the birds to be fed 'as usual, and charge it to me.'

Her writing has even given clues to the fact that the ebb and flow of urban bird populations is not necessarily just a modern phenomenon: 'I don't believe a word of it, that sparrow clubs are at an end and bird slaughter stopped. I saw a sensible diminution of birds in my last few weeks at Claydon over and above the extraordinary disap-pearance of the last two years. Some species have entirely disappeared. One wretched half-starved starling who came to my window to beg is the sole representative remaining of the splendid crown of starlings which used to sit or parade along the top of your church tower.'

Yet it was for an owl that the Lady of the Lamp devoted perhaps her greatest love. Rescuing it while in Greece from some boys who were tormenting it in 1850, she brought the bird back to England, and kept it with her in her bedroom at night, and carried it around with her in her pocket during the day. She named the owl Athena after the goddess of wisdom whose sacred symbol was the bird (the Latin name of the little owl, incidentally, is *Athene noctua*). Apt names ran in the Nightingale family. Florence's sister, born in Naples which is also known as Parthenope, was given the name... Parthenope. The nurse herself, unsurprisingly, was born in Florence.

QUOTE UNQUOTE

It is an important and popular fact that things are not always what they seem. For instance, on the planet Earth, man had always assumed that he was more intelligent than dolphins because he had achieved so much – the wheel, New York, war and so on – whilst all the dolphins had ever done is muck about in the water having a good time. But conversely, the dolphins had always believed that they were far more intelligent than man – for precisely the same reasons.
DOUGLAS ADAMS, writer and humourist

MEANWHILE, IN A FOREIGN LAND...

The vast majority of male birds don't have penises, mating by pressing their genitals against the females' in a 'cloacal kiss', but ostriches do have them, measuring up to 20cm in length, as do some ducks. The rather appropriately named stiff-tailed ducks of the Americas were known to have penises that even match that of the ostrich, until...

In September 2001, scientists came across one of nature's truly extraordinary sights: an Argentine lake duck with a 42.5cm penis. This remarkable organ, longer than the bird itself, rests naturally in a corkscrew shape for compactness, and has a brush-like tip at the end, probably to brush away another male's sperm from a female, so great is the sexual competition amongst the species.

ONCE UPON A TIME

Beasts that walked Britain before cameras were invented

	Last known individual
Spotted hyena	32,200 BC
Bison	25,650 BC
Woolly rhinoceros	22,350 BC
Wolverine	20,160 BC
Woolly mammoth	10,800 BC
Giant Irish elk	8,960 BC
Aurochs	1,000 BC
Brown bear	Probably 1st century AD although possibly until 8th century AD
Lynx	180 AD
Wolf	1690s AD

8 PLANTS THAT APPEAR TO BELONG TO SOMETHING ELSE

Colt's-foot
Dog's mercury
Dragon's-teeth
Hare's-ear
Leopard's-bane
Sheep's sorrel
Stork's-bill
Viper's-grass
And one that doesn't know WHAT it belongs to:
Dove's-foot crane's-bill

BACHELOR BOY

The Latin names of British animals and plants are generally descriptive of some aspect of the species, such as location, colour or habit. Yet occasionally a species is given a name based on unusual observations. Such is the case with the common chaffinch, whose Latin name is *Fringilla coelebs* – bachelor finch. Yet when we look out into our gardens or fields and see great flocks of the birds, we tend to see more females than males, particularly in the winter. If these birds are bachelors, it's not for want of choice, so how did the name come about?

The great taxonomist Linnaeus, who worked his way through a system of naming many European species, came from Sweden from where many chaffinches migrate south in the winter. They don't go far south, many of them ending up in Britain, but those that do tend to be female, for this is a species whose genders migrate slightly different distances. Linnaeus noticed that the chaffinches that remained in his home country during the cold season were predominantly male, so bachelor finches they became – much to the head-scratching of those in southern Europe.

A MOLE BY ANY OTHER NAME

Country names for the mole:
Crode
Heunt
Modywart
Mouldiwarp
Oont
Want

ANIMAL CRACKERS

In 2001, a welder from Huddersfield decided he wanted to get closer to the birds that lived near his home... so he turned himself into a walking bird table. Wearing a home-made construct on his head, he filled it with nuts, and settled down in some nearby woods. He didn't have long to wait. Within a few minutes, he heard a mighty crash, and found himself sprawled on the ground in agony. The table was shattered in pieces around him, and a grey squirrel, which had leapt from a nearby tree onto the makeshift buffet bar, was sprinting off into the woods. The squirrel ended up with a free meal, and the welder ended up in a neck brace.

The history of telescopes and binoculars

3500 BC

It was while cooking their local wildlife on sand that Phoenicians first discovered how to make glass. Sadly, no-one was able to use this discovery to help them watch wildlife for another 5,000 years, so they just kept on cooking it instead.

1608

The Dutchman and spectacle-maker Hans Lippershey of Holland is generally credited with the invention of the telescope, probably three or four times magnification, but it wasn't until the following year that the Italian scientist Galileo Galilei introduced the concept to astronomy, using his own telescope to see the craters of the moon, and discover sunspots, the rings of Saturn and the moons of Jupiter. His creation gave him a magnification of 30 times.

1825

It may seem strange, but it was over two centuries until someone thought of the idea of combining two telescopes into one optic instrument, thus improving on the limitations of monocular vision. Less strange is the fact that they were called binoculars: it was JP Lemiere who first patented the invention in this year.

1855

AS Herschel is believed to have invented a stereo-telescope in this year, an instrument with two telescopes, each with its objective directed to an eyepiece via mirrors or prisms for a greatly enhanced depth perception.

1894

The German optical industry began to kick off with great success, producing the first high quality modern binoculars based on the work of optical designer Ernst Abbe, glassmaker Otto Schott and instrument maker Carl Zeiss.

1935

Alexander Smakula's work helps invent antireflective coatings, increasing binocular light transmission by 50%.

1954

Tele-objective systems (two lens elements separated by air) are introduced, leading smaller binoculars and much improved image quality.

Late 1990s

People began to realise that by combining their digital cameras and their telescopes, they could get great photos of wildlife vast distances away, and the digiscoping industry is born. Today, we can watch and take photographs of wildlife without disturbing it, proudly displaying our results without having to shoot, trap, collect and stuff the creatures. But, of course, we're still cooking many of them.

THICK THISTLE STICKS

Say the following rapidly and without pause,
and win eternal self-admiration.

A flea and a fly flew in a flue,
Were imprisoned so what could they do?
Said the flea 'Let us fly!'
Said the fly 'Let us flee!'
So they flew through a flaw in the flue!

She sells seashells by the seashore
And the shells she sells are seashells I'm sure
So if she sells seashells by the seashore
Then I'm sure she sells seashore shells

Ann Anteater ate Andy Alligator's apples
So angry Andy Alligator ate Ann Anteater's ants

Thirty-three sly shy thrushes
Said that the sixth sheik's sixth sheep's sick

SAY THAT AGAIN?

Learning how to recognise birds by their calls takes experience, but
there are a few shortcuts. Some species have such distinctive calls
that they've been translated, so to speak, into English, such is their
familiarity. Here are a few of the best known:

Wet my lips	Quail
A little bit of bread and no cheese	Yellowhammer
Go back, go back	Red Grouse
Take two turns, Taffy	Woodpigeon
Tree, tree, tree, once more I come to thee	Pied Flycatcher
Nevermore	Raven (according to Edgar Allan Poe)

POST TRAUMATIC STRESS

It's not just dogs that attack postmen, as this list of news-making
creatures attests:
A goose
A mad cow
A pheasant
A shark (the postie was swimming)
Boo-boo the cat and Yogi the kitten

ALL GREEK TO ME

In January 2004, a *Guardian* sub-editor accidentally ran a spellchecker on a series of species' Latin names in an article on global warming. *Prunella modularis* (the dunnock) became *Pronely modularise*, the golden toad became *Buff* instead of *Bufo*, and the Spanish imperial eagle, once an *Aquila*, turned into an *Alleyway*. Magnificent.

Why stop there? Here are a few British butterfly species given a new spellchecked identity:

Ochlodes venata (large skipper) becomes *Occludes vent*
Erynnis tages (dingy skipper) becomes *Reins tags*
Papilio machaon (swallowtail) becomes *Papilla machine*
Colias croceus (clouded yellow) becomes *Coils crocus*
Pieris brassicae (large white) becomes *Piers brassiere*
Pieris napi (green-veined white) becomes *Piers nappy*
Lycaena phlaeas (small copper) becomes *Lycaena phallus*
Cupido minimus (small blue) becomes *Cupid minims*
Polyommatus icarus (common blue) becomes *Polymaths across*
Limenitis camilla (white admiral) becomes *Laments Camilla*
Apatura iris (purple emperor) becomes *Aperture iris*
Inachis io (peacock) becomes *Inches ion*
Boloria selene (small pearl-bordered fritillary) becomes *Bolero serene*
Melitaea cinxia (Glanville fritillary) becomes *Militia china*
Pararge aegeria (speckled wood) becomes *Prairie auger*
Erebia aethiops (Scotch argus) becomes *Erebus Ethiopia*

NATURE NOTES

I was born in September, and love it best of all the months. There is no heat, no hurry, no thirst and weariness in corn harvest as there is in the hay. If the season is late, as is usual with us, then mid-September sees the corn still standing in shock. The mornings come slowly. The earth is like a woman married and fading; she does not leap up with a laugh for the first fresh kiss of dawn, but slowly, quietly, unexpectantly likes watching the waking of each new day. The blue mist, like memory in the eyes of a neglected wife, never goes from the wooded hill, and only at noon creeps from the near hedges. There is no bird to put a song in the throat of the morning; only the crow's voice speaks during the day. Perhaps there is the regular breathing hust of the scythe – even the fretful jar of the mowing macine. But next day, in the morning, all is still again. The lying corn is wet, and when you have bound it, and life the heavy sheaf to make the stook, the tresses of oats wreathe round each other and droop mournfully.

DH Lawrence, *The White Peacock*

In 2003, workers in new, tall glass buildings in the city were noticing an unusual phenomenon. A surprisingly large number of woodcock, a bird of heavily wooded areas, were flying into the windows of their tower blocks. What on earth were they doing there?

Woodcock live in Britain all year round, their superbly camouflaged bodies helping them to blend in with their woodland environment. Usually only seen at dawn or dusk in spring when they make their 'roding' – display – flights, these secretive birds barely even make any sound, except the occasional soft grunt. Yet in the autumn, their numbers are augmented by migrational arrivals from the continent, some from as far away as Scandinavia. Woodcock are rather chunky, so the northern arrivals are probably exhausted by the time they arrive, and fail to notice that new buildings have been erected in their usual flight paths.

This knackered state also makes the usually elusive woodcock easy to approach, an unfortunate state for a gamebird to be in, as Gilbert White, the great 18th century naturalist, noticed. 'At present I do not know anybody near the seaside that will take the trouble to remark at what time of the moon woodcocks first come', he wrote. 'If I lived near the sea myself I would soon tell you more of the matter. One thing I used to observe when I was a sportsman was that there were times in which woodcocks were so sluggish and sleepy that they would drop again when flushed just before the spaniels, nay, just at the muzzle of a gun that had been fired at them'.

It seems that woodcocks and buildings are a bad mix in other parts of the world, too. The lakefront at Chicago has had more than 26,000 fatalities from birds flying into buildings over the last 20 years, no fewer than 500 of them being American woodcock. Oddly enough, most of them were female, and studies showed that their ovaries were highly developed, meaning they were just about to lay eggs. It has always been believed that American woodcock mate and lay their eggs in more or less the same place, but the Chicago data suggests that perhaps the females migrate elsewhere for the laying – until the buildings get in the way.

Meanwhile, in Toronto, advice has been put out on how to handle a stunned woodcock should you find it at the foot of a building. Whereas most birds can be put into a bag or box and taken to the vet, the Toronto wildlife centre recommends that as woodcocks can fly straight upwards, even in a small place, a second paper bag be put on top of them to avoid injury to both bird and carrier. And don't forget to put some air holes in.

NATURAL MYTHS

Porcupines shoot quills

Not true. Quills are just specially adapted hairs, and porcupines can
no more fire them than you could loose off part of your own barnet
at will. Porcupines use their quills as weapons by stabbing them into
their enemies, but they are able to release them once stuck into a
predator's flesh. Each quill is attached to the porcupine's body by
tissue, which is sheared upon impact, loosening the quill for
detachment. This could mean that the creature could be vulnerable
to infection from self-impaled tissue damage each time it attacks –
or, indeed, lands on the ground because porcupines frequently fall
out of trees – except for the fact that the quills come complete with
an antibiotic coating.

CRYPTIC CREATURES AND PUZZLING PLANTS

My first is in eagle but never in hawk
My second's in speaking but never in talk
My third is in dove but never in pigeon
My fourth is in teal and also in wigeon
My fifth is in throne and also in crown
My whole is a bird that can sure get you down
Answer on page 153

Answer on page 153

SITES FOR SORE EYES

It's summer, the sun is shining, and you want to see a swallowtail
butterfly. Understandable. The place to go is Hickling Broad,
restored in 2001 by the Norfolk Wildlife Trust, and now one of the
finest open water reserves in the country. A short boat ride to the
new 60ft Tree Tower provides excellent opportunities for watching
other wildlife, too, including roving marsh harriers, sizeable flocks
of wildfowl, and the chance of a glimpse of the secretive bittern.

Look out too, as you take the Water Trail, for the local Norfolk
hawker dragonfly, one of the reserve's specialities, as well as rare
species of stonewort and marsh orchid. The Broads are the reminder
of different times, the water-filled pits the remnants of hand-dug
peat excavations, used as fuel in the Middle Ages. But today, the
Broads are home to milk-parsley, the foodplant of the rare
swallowtail butterfly with its soaring courtship flight and
magnificent wingspan.

Cockatrice
Dragon's body with rooster's head. Prone to killing with noxious breath. Young naturalists might consider carrying a weasel while nature-watching as this is the only animal that can kill the cockatrice, should an individual turn nasty. Score: 20 pts.

HARD TO SWALLOW

Several mysteries of bird migration still surround us, yet at least today, thanks to advanced tracking techniques, we understand the basic principles and routes behind these feats of distance flight. It was not always so. Aristotle believed that redstarts turned into robins during the winter, thus explaining why he only saw each species in different seasons.

More recently, the great 18th century naturalist Gilbert White also found migration something to ponder. Although aware that many swallows disappeared to warmer climes during the cold months, he also believed that some preferred to hibernate in reedbeds through the winter, or through cold springs, rather than take on the full journey.

'It is worth remarking,' he wrote in 1774, 'that these birds are seen first about lakes and millponds; and it is also very particular, that if these early visitors happen to find frost and snow, as was the case of the two dreadful springs of 1770 and 1771, they immediately withdraw for a time. A circumstance like this is much more in favour of hiding than migration; since it is much more probable that a bird should retire to its hybernaculum just at hand, than return for a week or two only to warmer latitudes.'

Everyone wants to understand painting. Why is there no attempt to understand the song of the birds?
PABLO PICASSO, artist

WHO'D BE A GLANVILLE?

There's not much good fortune in being a Glanville. The Glanville fritillary is one of Britain's rarest butterflies, found on the south coast of the Isle of Wight. A small colony turned up on the Hampshire coast in the 1990s, but attempts to introduce the species elsewhere on the mainland have not been successful.

Perhaps it has inherited its misfortune from Lady Glanville, who gave it its name. Lady Glanville was a fanatical lepidopterist of the 18th century, who collected hundreds upon hundreds of adults and larvae for naturalists to study.

Such was her fervour, that she would be seen beating the hedges for 'a parcel of wormes', with an enthusiasm shared by few entomologists of the day. Butterflies were not considered as interesting as other families: 'None but those deprived of their Senses would go in Pursuit of butterflyes' wrote one contemporary entomologist.

This perceived 'lack of sense' was to stand against her. Upon her death, her relatives successfully voided her will on the grounds that anybody who chased butterflies was clearly not sane enough to have made one.

LEARNING FROM NATURE

Don't get too close to the bombardier beetle. It can squirt rapid-fire jets of boiling liquid at its enemies at a very high pressure, although those enemies do tend to be ants, frogs and spiders. Its firing action, however, has got aviation specialists interested. The beetle's unique natural combustion technique – known as pulse combustion – could help them solve the problem of re-igniting a gas turbine aircraft engine which has cut out, particularly at great heights where the outside temperature is very low.

Current research is focusing on understanding the beetle's heart-shaped miniature combustion chamber, which is less than one millimetre long. Simulations for a larger chamber around a few centimetres long are being prepared, in which gases are ignited by raising the chamber's surface temperature. It is thought that the beetle's unique nozzle shape might also help the scientists develop more accurate squirting power.

NATURE NOTES

On the tenth of April I heard the cuckoo, sitting in Sussex, my back against an oak. A grey mare at grass shared the place with me. Here and hereabout English and Norman had met and fought: there had been din and slaughter. Nothing had changed but men. The oak grew in the same way; the cuckoo came punctually about the second week in April, laid her eggs in other birds' nests and flew away. Yet even that must have had a beginning: there must have been a first time that a cuckoo's two notes broke the quiet of a spring morning, a first time that a cuckoo laid in another bird's nest. Why, among all birds so devoted to their young, should there be this one exception? What a process of mind, you would think, must have replaced instinct, before it could become in its turn instinctive. It is a subterfuge characteristic of the brain of man.

Adrian Bell, *Men and the Fields*, 1939

MEANWHILE, IN A FOREIGN LAND...

Climate change could be the doom of many a creature as prehistory teaches us, but the threat it poses to the alpine water skink is more unusual than most.

The skink bears its young live, but unlike other live-bearing creatures, the sex of the young is determined by the temperature in which the pregnant female lives. The warmer the environment, the more likely the offspring are to be male, up to about 32°C, at which not a single female is born.

Living as it does in alpine areas, the water skink's habitat temperature is therefore at just the right balance to produce the optimum percentage of male and female young. Yet if predictions are correct, and the region warms up in the coming decades, then the female water skink may become a thing of the past... as would the species.

WILL YOU GET THE BILL?

Beak or bill: which is the correct name for each bird? If you want to play it safe, go for beak each time, as this is the actual name given to the skull extension that all birds have. Beaks owned by web-footed birds and pigeons, as well as those that are particularly long, slender or flattened, tend to be known as bills.

Of course, if you should decide to kill the bird, then the confusion ends. The bill is the one who catches you, while the beak is the one who slaps you in jail.

10 ODDLY NAMED BRITISH MOTHS

The uncertain
The confused
The magpie
The lackey
The iron prominent
The true lover's knot
The Hebrew character
The old lady
The angle shades
The Mother Shipton

SIMIAN STARS

Cheetah – The chimpanzee who accompanied Tarzan on his adventures. In 1986, Maureen O'Sullivan, who played Jane, revealed that Cheetah had had the hots for Johnny Weismuller and had to be restrained during her scenes with him to prevent sudden bursts of jealousy. She visited him in later life, and he spat in her face.

Marcel – Ross's monkey from the sitcom *Friends*. He was sacked from the series after continual vomiting of live worms on set.

Judy – The chimpanzee from *Daktari*. A close friend of Clarence the cross-eyed lion in the jungle-based animal doctor series, Judy was a trained chimp who responded to up to 75 hand signals. She was potty-trained, although tended to used more toilet paper than necessary.

CJ – The orangutan who got close to Clint Eastwood in *Every Which Way But Loose*, and *Any Which Way You Can*, and closer still to Bo Derek in *Tarzan, The Ape Man*. Born at Dallas Zoo in 1971, he was put up for adoption at the age of seven at which time he was purchased by Boone Narr, a head animal trainer and Bill Gage. He liked cookies and milk before going to bed. Reportedly, CJ received a yearly fee of US$500,000.

QUOTE UNQUOTE

No-one else seems to have seen the sparkle on the brook, or heard the music at the hatch, or to have felt back through the centuries; and when I try to describe these things to them they look at me with stolid incredulity. No-one seems to understand how I get food from the clouds, nor what there was in the night, nor why it is not so good to look at it out of a window.
RICHARD JEFFRIES, naturalist and poet

Which of the following is not a type of dragonfly:
Hawker
Chaser
Skimmer
Flicker
Darter?
Answer on page 153.

WHAT'S UP, DOCK?

Anyone who's spent any time in the countryside will have experienced the wrath of the stinging nettle. But what actually is happening to you when the nettle attacks?

Each sting is a hollow hair stiffened by silica with a swollen base that contains venom. The tip of this hair is very brittle and when brushed against, no matter how lightly, it breaks off exposing a sharp point that penetrates the skin. It was once thought that the main constituent of the sting was formic acid, the chemical used by ants, but although this acid is present, the main chemicals are histamine, acetylcholine and 5-hydroxytryptamine (serotonin). There is a fourth ingredient that has not yet been identified.

Yet while nature takes away with one hand, so it gives with another. Dock, which often grows in the neighbourhood of nettles, contains chemicals in its leaves that neutralise the sting and cool the skin.

NATURE NOTES

Consider that the whale has nothing that can properly be called a neck; on the contrary, where his head and body seem to join, there, in that very place, is the thickest part of him. Remember, also, that the surgeon must operate from above, some eight or ten feet intervening between him and his subject, and that subject almost hidden in a discoloured, rolling, and oftentimes tumultuous and bursting sea. Bear in mind, too, that under these untoward circumstances he has to cut many feet deep in the flesh; and in that subterraneous manner, without so much as getting one single peep into the ever-contracting gash thus made, he must skilfully steer clear of all adjacent, interdicted parts, and exactly divide the spine at a critical point hard by its insertion into the skull. Do you not marvel, then, at Stubb's boast, that he demanded but ten minutes to behead a sperm whale?

Herman Melville, *Moby Dick*

ARTHEI TEKINTHAPIS

Scientists take their jobs very seriously. But sometimes, just sometimes, they let the mask slip. Here is a list of Latin names given to creatures whose discoverers were in a more flippant mood than usual at the time:

Agra cadabra .... a carabid
Apopyllus now ....a spider
Ba humbugi ....a Fijian snail
Cyclocephala nodanotherwon ....a scarab beetle
Dissup irae..fossil fly, very hard to see
Eubetia bigaulae ....a moth, yes it is, you betcha by golly
Ittibittium ....a tiny mollusc
Heerz lukenatcha ....a braconid
Kamera lens..a protist
La cucaracha ....a pyralid
Notnops, Taintnops, Tisentnops ....spiders

> They were originally in the genus *Nops*, but were separated out into these new genera in 1994

Pieza kake ....a fly
Ptomaspis, Dikenaspis, Ariaspis ....types of fish

> Remove the '-aspis' to get it

Tabanus rhizonshine..a horse fly
Verae peculya ....a braconid
Vini vidivici ....a parrot
Ytu brutus..a water beetle

SITES FOR SORE EYES

The Isles of Scilly are like nowhere else in the world: a microcosm of diversity, a unique way of life, and a beautiful, unspoilt natural environment. Auks, petrels, shearwaters and fulmars breed around the archipelago, while bats, which do not hibernate due to the warm climate, can be seen feeding all year round.

The sea life is, of course, impressive. Porpoises, dolphins and the occasional whale are to be looked out for, along with the spectacular sun fish, easily seen as the water is so clear around the islands. Land-based mammals are few and far between, but the eastern isles are very good for seals, and if you're very lucky, you might catch a glimpse of the endemic Scilly shrew. The heady scent of the narcissus crop fills the winter air, while three types of adder's-tongue fern grace St Agnes Island. The four inhabited islands can be explored via a series of permissive paths, and the whole natural spectacle is looked after by The Isles of Scilly Wildlife Trust.

Some plants beginning with B in the works of Shakespeare:

Captain: 'Tis thought the king is dead; we will not stay. The BAY-trees in our country are all wither'd And meteors fright the fixed stars of heaven.
Richard II, Act 2, Scene 4

Maria: Get ye all three into the BOX-tree: Malvolio's coming down this walk: he has been yonder i' the sun practising behaviour to his own shadow this half hour: observe him, for the love of mockery; for I know this letter will make a contemplative idiot of him.
Twelfth Night, Act 2, Scene 5

Cordelia: Alack, 'tis he: why, he was met even now As mad as the vex'd sea; singing aloud; Crown'd with rank fumiter and furrow-weeds, With BUR-DOCKS, hemlock, nettles, cuckoo-flowers, Darnel, and all the idle weeds that grow In our sustaining corn.
King Lear, Act 4, Scene 4

Duke Vincentio: We have strict statutes and most biting laws… Now, as fond fathers, Having bound up the threatening twigs of BIRCH, Only to stick it in their children's sight For terror, not to use, in time the rod Becomes more mock'd than fear'd; so our decrees, Dead to infliction, to themselves are dead; And liberty plucks justice by the nose; The baby beats the nurse, and quite athwart Goes all decorum.
Measure for Measure, Act 1, Scene 3

Second Carrier: Peas and BEANS are as dank here as a dog, and that is the next way to give poor jades the bots: this house is turned upside down since Robin Ostler died.
King Henry IV, Part 1, Act 2, Scene 1

Flute: Most radiant Pyramus, most lily-white of hue, Of colour like the red rose on triumphant BRIER, Most brisky juvenal and eke most lovely Jew, As true as truest horse that yet would never tire, I'll meet thee, Pyramus, at Ninny's tomb.
A Midsummer Night's Dream, Act 3, Scene 1

Pistol: Elves, list your names; silence, you airy toys. Cricket, to Windsor chimneys shalt thou leap: Where fires thou find'st unraked and hearths unswept, There pinch the maids as blue as BILBERRY: Our radiant queen hates sluts and sluttery.
The Merry Wives of Windsor, Act 5, Scene 5

Rosalind: There is a man haunts the forest, that abuses our young plants with carving 'Rosalind' on their barks; hangs odes upon hawthorns and elegies on BRAM-BLES, all, forsooth, deifying the name of Rosalind: if I could meet that fancy-monger I would give him some good counsel, for he seems to have the quotidian of love upon him.
As You Like It, Act 3, Scene 2

MEANWHILE, IN FOREIGN WATERS

We may be used to the discovery of small and microscopic creatures new to science, but how about a creature larger in size than man? Four thousand feet down in the Pacific Ocean, a most unusual new jellyfish has recently been found. Measuring up to three metres in diameter, 'Big Red' has arms instead of tentacles, with which it presumably catches its food. Yet what does it eat, and why has it bucked the usual jellyfish trend? No-one's sure yet. Not only has only one specimen been caught, its deep red pigmentation hasn't allowed scientists to get a good look at the contents of its stomach yet.

EVER FELT GULLED?

New-year twitches are a staple part of the list-keeping birder's diet. Every year brings the start of a brand new list, so rarities that have hung around beyond Christmas are worth chasing down as early as possible in January to make sure they appear on that year's list. At Titchwell in North Norfolk, for example, a black-winged stilt, very rare to Britain, has been resident since the early 1990s. Nicknamed Sammy, he has provided birdwatchers of all types with an unusual tick each year... but many like to 'get' him as quickly as possible, just in case poor Sammy pegs it.

Sometimes the new year twitch doesn't go so well, however. In 2000, many birders decided to see in the new millennium by popping down to Aldeburgh in Suffolk where a graceful ivory gull had been ghosting its way up and down the beach for about three weeks. They'd already ticked him off for 1999, now to put him on the 2000 list. Sadly, it wasn't to be. The gull wasn't there, frightened off, apparently, by the celebratory fireworks the night before.

NATURAL SAYINGS FROM AROUND THE WORLD

The beetle in his hole is a Sultan – Egypt
Before fording the river, do not curse the alligator's mother – Haiti
He who marries a wolf often looks towards the forest – Basque
Friends tie their purses with a spider's thread – Italy
The interested friend is a swallow on the roof – France
It is not enough for a man to know how to ride, he must know
how to fall – Mexico
In the ant's house dew is a deluge – Iran
Only an owl knows the worth of an owl – India
One crow never pecks out another's eyes – Romania
Only the nightingale can understand the rose – Bulgaria

NATURE NOTES

Everybody is still running towards the Regent's Park, for the purpose of passing half an hour with the Hippopotamus. The animal itself repays public curiosity with a yawn of indifference, or throws cold water on the ardour of his visitors, by suddenly plunging into his bath, and splashing every one within five yards of him.

Much disappointment has been expressed at the Hippopotamus, in consequence of its not being exactly up to the general idea of a sea-horse, and many hundreds go away grumbling every day, because the brute is not so equestrian in appearance as could be desired. Many persons thought the Hippopotamus was a regular sea-horse, kept expressly for running in harness in a sea-captain's gig; but as the creature turns out to be very like a hog, there are many who go the entire animal in finding fault with him.

Punch, December 1850
The article referred to the new arrival at London Zoo

THE BOTTOMLESS PIT

Ant-lions were first reliably recorded in Britain in 1931, but it is only in more recent years that the creatures have been more regularly sighted, principally on the East Anglian coast.

Ant-lion is the name given to the larvae of the *Myrmeleontidae* family, insects that resemble small damselflies in flight. The larvae corkscrew themselves backwards into sand, leaving a funnel-shaped pit above them. There they lie in wait with just their pincers showing. Passing insects fall into the pit, and struggle to get out due to the loose sand grains that make the pit wall and sometimes, while on the edge of the pit, they are bombarded by sand flicked at them by the ant-lion's head, until they lose their footing and fall in.

Once their prey is at the bottom of the pit, the ant-lions grab it with their pincers and proceed to infuse enymes into its body. These enzymes kill the insect, and dissolve their soft tissue into liquid, which the ant-lion then simply sucks in. Because the larva digests it meal so efficiently, it has no need of an anus, bringing up any residual solids as a pellet once it turns into an adult.

QUOTE UNQUOTE

I want meadows red in tone and trees painted in blue. Nature has no imagination.
CHARLES BAUDELAIRE, French poet

Number, in thousands, of grey seals annually tagged electronically by St Andrews University to learn more about their habits and environment

A NEW SPECIES

The rare five-legged elephant that has scientists baffled:

FILMS FOR WILDLIFE-WATCHERS

The Mouse that Roared (1959)
Sweet Bird Of Youth (1962)
The Birds (1963)
Cat Ballou (1965)
Paper Lion (1968)
The Lion in Winter (1968)
The Eagle has Landed (1976)
The Deer Hunter (1978)
Raging Bull (1980)
The Fox and the Hound (1981)
Night Hawk (1981)
Never Cry Wolf (1983)
Gorillas in the Mist (1988)
Dances with Wolves (1990)
The Silence of the Lambs (1991)
The Lion King (1994)
Wag the Dog (1997)

WHY FUNGI AREN'T PLANTS

- Fungi cell walls are made of chitin, not cellulose as in plants.

- Fungi have no chlorophyll so cannot make their own food.

- Fungi digest food outside their bodies by excreting enzymes that ooze out of the fungus body, and then absorb digested material through the cell walls.

- Fungal cells are simple in structure and function: most are tubular in shape, connected end to end and thereafter deploy as circular growths of hair-like material.

- Fungi reproduce by producing spores which are little more than a fragment of the parent fungus cell.

- Fungi have no roots, stems, leaves or bark.

- Fungi reproduce by producing spores which are little more than a fragment of the parent fungus cell.

As a result of these and other differences, biologists created a third kingdom of living organisms – the Fungi *– in 1784. Previously, biologists such as Linnaeus had lumped them together with plants.*

QUOTE UNQUOTE

We hope that, when the insects take over the world, they will remember with gratitude how we took them along on all our picnics.
BILL VAUGHAN, US journalist

GONE DOWN IN NATURAL HISTORY

Wildlife named after leaders
Caligula – a moth
Jenghizkhan – a dinosaur
Paroxyna cleopatra – a fruit fly
Parides montezuma – a swallowtail
Mammuthus jeffersonii – a mammoth. Named after
US President Thomas Jefferson
Mandelia – a sea slug. Named after Nelson Mandela
Anophthalmus hitleri – a blind cave beetle. It was named in the
1930s by admirer Hitler. Today, it is very rare because collectors of
Nazi memorabilia seem to think they need one
Sequoia – the redwood. Named after
Cherokee chief Sequoyah
Spartacus – a leaf bug
Washingtonia – a fan palm

YOU'RE SURE OF A BIG SURPRISE

Whereas most British birds somehow vaguely look as if they belong to this country, the golden pheasant is a species that simply oozes international roots. Admitted to the British list in 1971, thanks to its successful colonisation from escaped individuals, it can be found in around half a dozen sites in Britain, chiefly in East Anglia, the South Downs and areas around Poole Harbour.

It's a beautiful bird, found in dense, dark woodland (it roosts in trees at night), the closest it can get to its native Chinese bamboo plantations. The male is unmistakable: very brightly coloured with a yellow crown and lower back, dark wings and upper neck, red underparts and long finely barred tail. Although attempts have been made to introduce it to Europe, only the British population, an accidental introduction, has succeeded. Another species, the Lady Amherst's pheasant, has also taken root, this time in Bedfordshire.

Interestingly, our own pheasant is not an original native of Britain, first introduced as a game bird from Asia in around the 12th century.

MEDIEVAL MAGIC

How to pronounce the first 12 lines of Chaucer's beautiful introduction to *The Canterbury Tales*:

Whan that Aprille with his shoores soote/*Wan thot A'prill with his sure-es so-tuh*

The drought of March hath perced to the roote/*The drewgt of March hath pear-said to the row-tuh*

And bathed every vein in swich liquor/*And ba-thed every vane in sweech lee-coor*

Of which vertu engendred is the flour/*Of wheech ver-too en-jen-dred is the flu-er*

When Zephyrus eek with his sweete breeth/*When Zeph-er-us ache with his sway-tuh breath*

Inspired hath in every holt and heeth/*In-spear-ed hath in every holt and heth*

The tendre croppes and the yonge sun/*The tawn-dray crop-pays and the young-gay soan*

Hath in the ram his halve cours yronne/*Hath in the rahm his hall-vey coors e-rown*

And smale fowles maken melodye/*And smal-ay foe-lays mock-en mel-oh-dee-uh*

That slepen all the night with open eye/*That slep-en all the neekdt with open ee-ah*

So priketh hem nature in hir courages/*So prick-eth him nah-tour in hear core-ahj-ez*

Thanne longen folke to goon pilgrimages/*Thah-nay lon-gen folk to goen-on pilgrim-ahj-ez*

NATURE NOTES

While standing on a dunghill

Good farmyard manure. I take large spadefuls of the stuff, like great slabs of chocolate cake, and throw them into a cart. As we open up the dunghill it begins to steam and its excellent odour becomes somewhat stronger. Various insects alight upon it. I cannot see the very small ones, of course, but would like to know the full insectitude activity. I observe one that always seems to be sharpening its forceps like a man in front of a joint – he of the brown wings. Also he of the beaked and vampire face. He of the dumb-bell body. He of the sleek and jet-black mail. I lift up their mountain of food into the cart, drive it off, and then throw it on the field. After which I climb on to another huge dunghill and fill up the cart again. And I must say I never felt better employed.

John Stewart Collis, *The Worm forgives the Plough*

COATS OF ANIMALS

County council coats of arms that incorporate animals include:

Berkshire

Cornwall

Kent

Oxford

Warwickshire

Wiltshire

CRYPTIC CREATURES AND PUZZLING PLANTS

Unravel the following:
NELT
Answer on page 153

MEANWHILE, IN FOREIGN WATERS...

The sailfish is considered to be the fastest fish in the world over short distances: it has been recorded travelling at 68mph. Growing up to 10ft in length, it can lay as many as 4.8 million eggs in one breeding season.

LEARN THE LINGO

Serious birders have found ways of shortening many species' names for easy conversation, and rapid paging and texting of information. Here is a list of some of the abbreviations:

Barwit	Bar-tailed godwit. Black-tailed godwits are known as 'Blackwits'.
Blackback	Either of the greater or lesser black-backed gulls.
Capper	Capercaillie. The abbreviation shows the correct pronunciation of the first half of the bird's name.
Commic	Either common or arctic tern, two species that are notoriously difficult to separate.
Fly	Flycatcher. Spotted flycatcher is often abbreviated to spot fly.
Greatspot	Great spotted woodpecker.
Gropper	Grasshopper warbler.
Icky	Icterine warbler.
Mickey Ringo	Little ringed plover.
Millow	Marsh or willow tit. These two birds were only recognised as different species in 1897.
P G Tips	Pallas' grasshopper warbler.
Razormot	A collection of guillemot and razorbills.
Ringtail	A female or immature hen or Montagu's harrier.
Sand	Any of the many species of sandpiper.
Sprog	House sparrow.
Twitcher	Type of birdwatcher who travels great distances to see rare birds at the drop of a hat. Few birders call themselves twitchers, so if a non-birdwatcher uses the term generically to describe the species, this can cause great offence.

FROGS ARE FUNNY

A chicken walks into a library, goes up to the counter and clucks 'book, book, book'.

The librarian is bemused, but hands over three books without thinking. The chicken tucks them under its wing, and waddles out. The next day it's back – 'book, book, book' – and the next, and the next, each time going off with three books.

By the fifth day, the librarian is so curious, he decides to follow the chicken. He follows it down the road to the pond on the village green, where he watches the chicken hand the books over to a frog, who leafs through them croaking: 'Reddit, reddit, reddit'.

MAYBE ITS MOTHER LOVES IT

Quite possibly the hardest of Britain's creatures to harbour feelings of fondness for is the hagfish. This curious sea creature resembles a pinkish or greyish eel, with short tentacles around its mouth, and glands along its side. For a couple of hundred million years, the hagfish has cheerfully lived out an existence chewing its way into the bodies of ill or dead fish or marine worms, and eating its way out again.

The glamour doesn't stop there. Try catching a hagfish, and you'll find out what the glands are for: they secrete copious amounts of mucous-like slime that has most predators gummed up in the mouth, or recoiling in horror. The hagfish is even capable of sneezing out slime from its mouth.

Should you happen to capture one, however, and slip it into a bucket, don't turn your back. The hagfish is capable of tying itself into a knot, which it uses as a balancing base to force itself over the top of the bucket. Thanks to its slippery body, it then simply slides itself out of the knot again, and makes a break for freedom.

Hard to love, impossible not to admire.

ANIMAL CRACKERS

Queen Christina of Sweden (1626–1689) had a very strong loathing for fleas. This was particularly unfortunate, as they tended to infest her bedroom. In desperation, she had built a miniature four-inch cannon, with which she would fire tiny cannonballs at them. Records do not tell us whether she ever hit one.

SITES FOR SORE EYES

Sometimes an entire island can become a naturalist's paradise, and the Isle of Eigg, of the Inner Hebrides, is no exception. Accessible by ferry, visitors have a reasonable chance of watching minke whales as they cross between the months of July and September. Once on the island itself, wildflower meadows, hazel woods and heather moors open up, while the craggy outline plays host to eagles.

This is one of the great joys of the island: so many habitats within such close walking distance of each other. The bird list is just short of 200 species – impressive for such a small isle – and the plantlife is rich, including 12 species of orchid and 20 nationally rare bryophytes. With otters, 18 species of butterfly, the pygmy shrew and the island wood mouse, brought over by the Norse raiders, Eigg, now co-managed by the Scottish Wildlife Trust, offers a stunning variety of sights and discoveries.

QUOTE UNQUOTE

The greatness of a nation and its moral progress can be judged by the way its animals are treated.
MAHATMA GANDHI, Indian statesman

NATURE NOTES

The same evening, under the same beeches on the edge of the wood while the grey slugs came down from the top of the beeches where they spend the day, I saw the wedding of the ants. Those which are to couple have wings and the couples join in the air; but as soon as the male has clasped the female, their wings are entangled, their nerves are agitated, and the two entwined insects turn over and over and fall. The weddings I saw had been exalted very high above the trees, the golden rain fell from leaf to leaf with the sound of a shower, and as each couple touched the ground the two lovers, immediately unjoined, sprang up like the drops of a cascade and flew off rapidly and alone towards the sun and towards death. Strange and almost terrifying vision! I am very proud to have seen the sight and I despise myself for loving with so many precautions, turns and ruses, when I think how the ants give their whole life for life, and only separate for the females to carry the fertilised treasure to the ant-hill and for the males to die. I am inclined to think the males die immediately and that only the females fly up; but I was intoxicated at participating in this mystery, and as soon as I understood it I began to reflect in order to understand it better.

Remy de Gourmont, *Selections* (translated by Richard Aldington)

Number, in thousands, of inter-connected nests in the largest known 45
ant colony. It was found on Hokkaido, Japan

THE ROMAN GAMES

Ever wondered why both the animal and plant kingdoms boast families of fritillaries? The word comes from the Latin *Fritillus*, meaning dice box, and the shape of the fritillary flower bears a strong resemblance to the dice boxes used in Roman times. As the flower has a chequered pattern, the butterfly then probably got its name from its similar markings.

There are some, however, who believe that the butterfly, which has a bouncing, fluttery flight, was so named because it flies like the dice as they bounce around in the box. There are others, too, who believe that the flower gained its name not so much from the shape of the dice box, as the spotted nature of its contents. Yet another group prefers to translate *Fritillus* as chequerboard, arguing that both flower and butterfly look like one. What is certain, however, is that each family name has its roots in the games of old Rome.

THE WILD BUNCH

Original line-up of The Animals in 1963:

Eric Burdon (vocals)
Hilton Valentine (guitar)
Chas Chandler (bass)
Alan Price (keyboards)
John Steel (drums)

KNOW YOUR BATS

If you closed your eyes and picked a random name from the world list of mammal species, you'd have a 25% chance of coming up with a bat. In Britain, the trend is reflected: we have 15 species and a couple of occasional visitors (out of approximately 60 non-marine mammal species), although telling them apart as they flit above your head is one of the hardest aspects of nature-watching.

Technology is helping, however. Bat detectors, which measure the frequency of bat calls as they navigate their way around the night skies, are revolutionising bat recording and monitoring. In the early days, they simply converted the high-frequency calls into sound, which still meant you needed to know what you were listening to. Today, however, you can get detectors that produce visual sonographs of the sound, which at a glance tell you which species you caught a brief glimpse of as it flicked by. In part thanks to this technology, the common pipistrelle was split into two different species in 1995. One emits sounds at 55kHz, the other at 45kHz. Easy, really.

WHAT'S SO LADYLIKE ABOUT THE LADYBIRD?

Of the thousands of species of ladybird found around the world, over 40 can be regularly seen in Britain, of which 26 are recognisable as ladybirds. Often named after the number of spots on their wing-cases (elytra), the vast majority of our species are carnivorous, their food of choice being aphids, which make them gardeners' favourites. The vegetarians feed on mildews.

Many insects are brightly coloured as a means of warning predators that they're not particularly good to eat – a sort of wildlife danger symbol – and ladybirds are no exception. They use a defence mechanism known as reflex bleeding, releasing drops of their pungent blood from their legs onto the tongue or beak of their devourer. This does little good to the individual that gets chomped, but its predator will think twice before feasting on ladybirds again.

The average ladybird will consume 5,500 aphids in its year-long life.

So what's so ladylike about all this? The insect's red body reminded many of medieval paintings depicting the Virgin Mary wearing a red cloak, while the spots of the common seven-spot ladybird were seen to represent her seven joys and seven sorrows. Add in the fact that the insect can fly, and 'Our Lady's bird' became its early vernacular name.

THE VULGAR TONGUE

The word 'vulgar' may have pretty derogatory connotations today, but its root lies in the Latin for 'common', back in the empirical days when to be common was, well, a fairly derogatory thing to be. As a result, many of our most beautiful plants and animals rejoice in scientific vulgarity, even though some are not as 'vulgar' as they used to be:

Polygala vulgaris ....Common milkwort
Clinopodium vulgare ....Wild basil
Sciurus vulgaris ....Red squirrel
Primula vulgaris ....Primrose
Sturnus vulgaris ....Starling
Echium vulgare ....Viper's bugloss

QUOTE UNQUOTE

Weeds are flowers too, once you get to know them.
EEYORE, a donkey

11 FILMS THAT EXPLOIT OUR MISCONCEPTIONS OF THE ANIMAL KINGDOM WHILE MAKING A MINT FOR STUDIO EXECS WHO SHOULD REALLY KNOW BETTER

Eight-legged Freaks
Spiders are proven to be man's greatest enemy

Jaws 3
Having made the point twice before, Hollywood rams home the
fact that sharks are man's greatest enemy

Them
In which man's greatest enemy is revealed to be ants

The Birds
Man's greatest enemy turns out to be airborne

Curse of the Wolfman
Man becomes his own greatest enemy with the help
of the animal kingdom

The Swarm
Turns out that man's greatest enemy is an insect after all…

Piranha
…or a fish…

Lake Placid
…or a reptile

Cats and Dogs
Shown to be each other's greatest enemy…

The Ghost and the Darkness and *Cujo*
…but sometimes man's greatest enemy, too

REAL JOBS HELD BY JOHNNY MORRIS

Many young children of the 1960s and 1970s grew up believing
that Johnny Morris was a zoo-keeper, rather than a TV presenter.
His show, *Animal Magic*, featured lemurs, the artwork of Keith
Shackleton, and a host of creatures that appeared to have
conversations with Johnny as he sat with them in their cages. But
his Doolittle act came relatively late in life. Before the days of
Animal Magic, he had been a:

Solicitor's assistant
Timekeeper on a building site
Salesman
Farm manager in Wiltshire
Hot Chestnut Man – telling yarns on TV in the 1950s

The Roman Pliny the Elder (Gaius Plinius Secundus) was one of the greatest of the early natural historians. His *Natural History* encyclopaedia of 77 AD was the first of its kind, a 37-volume collection of work that set out to record all the creatures of the known world.

With a further 75 books to his name, this early scientist had a curiosity about the natural world that filled his life, and caused his death. In this extraordinary account, his nephew, Pliny the Younger, explains how Pliny's rampant thirst for knowledge drove him to a fatal study of the erupting Vesuvius at Pompeii:

'He was at Misenum in his capacity as commander of the fleet on the 24 August [79 AD], when between two and three in the afternoon my mother drew his attention to a cloud of unusual size and appearance. He had had a sunbath, then a cold bath, and was reclining after dinner with his books. He called for his shoes and climbed up to where he could get the best view of the phenomenon. The cloud was rising from a mountain-at such a distance we couldn't tell which, but afterwards learned that it was Vesuvius. I can best describe its shape by likening it to a pine tree. It rose into the sky on a very long 'trunk' from which spread some 'branches'. I imagine it had been raised by a sudden blast, which then weakened, leaving the cloud unsupported so that its own weight caused it to spread sideways. Some of the cloud was white, in other parts there were dark patches of dirt and ash. The sight of it made the scientist in my uncle determined to see it from closer at hand.

'He ordered a boat made ready. He offered me the opportunity of going along, but I preferred to study – he himself happened to have set me a writing exercise. As he was leaving the house he was brought a letter from Tascius' wife Rectina, who was terrified by the looming danger. Her villa lay at the foot of Vesuvius, and there was no way out except by boat. She begged him to get her away. He changed his plans. The expedition that started out as a quest for knowledge now called for courage. He launched the quadriremes and embarked himself, a source of aid for more people than just Rectina, for that delightful shore was a populous one. He hurried to a place from which others were fleeing, and held his course directly into danger. Was he afraid? It seems not, as he kept up a continuous observation of the various movements and shapes of that evil cloud, dictating what he saw.

'Ash was falling onto the ships now, darker and denser the closer they went. Now it was bits of pumice, and rocks that were blackened and burned and shattered by the fire. Now the sea is shoal; debris from the mountain blocks the shore. He paused for a moment wondering whether to turn back as the helmsman urged him. "Fortune helps the brave," he said, "Head for Pomponianus."

'At Stabiae, on the other side of the bay, Pomponianus had loaded up his ships even before the danger arrived, though it was visible and indeed extremely close, once it intensified. He planned to put out as soon as the contrary wind let up. That very wind carried my uncle right in, and he embraced the frightened man and gave him comfort and courage. In order to lessen the other's fear by showing his own unconcern he asked to be taken to the baths. He bathed and dined, carefree or at least appearing so (which is equally impressive). Meanwhile, broad sheets of flame were lighting up many parts of Vesuvius; their light and brightness were the more vivid for the darkness of the night. To alleviate people's fears my uncle claimed that the flames came from the deserted homes of farmers who had left in a panic with the hearth fires still alight. Then he rested, and gave every indication of actually sleeping; people who passed by his door heard his snores, which were rather resonant since he was a heavy man. The ground outside his room rose so high with the mixture of ash and stones that if he had spent any more time there escape would have been impossible. He got up and came out, restoring himself to Pomponianus and the others who had been unable to sleep. They discussed what to do, whether to remain under cover or to try the open air. The buildings were being rocked by a series of strong tremors, and appeared to have come loose from their foundations and to be sliding this way and that. Outside, however, there was danger from the rocks that were coming down, light and fire-consumed as these bits of pumice were. Weighing the relative dangers they chose the outdoors; in my uncle's case it was a rational decision, others just chose the alternative that frightened them the least.

'They tied pillows on top of their heads as protection against the shower of rock. It was daylight now elsewhere in the world, but there the darkness was darker and thicker than any night. But they had torches and other lights. They decided to go down to the shore, to see from close up if anything was possible by sea. But it remained as rough and uncooperative as before. Resting in the shade of a sail he drank once or twice from the cold water he had asked for. Then came an smell of sulfur, announcing the flames, and the flames themselves, sending others into flight but reviving him. Supported by two small slaves he stood up, and immediately collapsed. As I understand it, his breathing was obstructed by the dust-laden air, and his innards, which were never strong and often blocked or upset, simply shut down. When daylight came again two days after he died, his body was found untouched, unharmed, in the clothing that he had had on. He looked more asleep than dead.'

Perhaps a heavy buzzard may rise, flapping, from its nest on the moor, or pounce from a crag in the direction of any water-birds that may be about the springs and pools in the hills. There is no other sound, unless it be the hum of the gnats in the hot sunshine. There is an aged man in the district, however, who hears more than this, and sees more than people below would, perhaps, imagine. An old shepherd has the charge of four rain gauges which are set up on four ridges – desolate, misty spots, sometimes below and often above the clouds. He visits each once a month and notes down what these gauges record; and when the tall old man, with his staff, passes out of sight into the cloud, or among the cresting rocks, it is a striking thought that science has set up a tabernacle in these wildernesses and found a priest among the shepherds. That old man has seen and heard wonderful things – has trod upon rainbows, and been waited upon by a a dim retinue of spectral mists. He has seen the hail and the lightning go forth as from under his hand, and has stood in the sunshine, listening to the thunder growling, and the tempest bursting beneath his feet. He well knows the silence of the hills, and all the solemn ways in which that silence is broken. The stranger, however, coming hither on a calm sunny day may well fancy that a silence like this can never be broken.

Harriet Martineau, *Guide to Windermere*

STRANGELY OMITTED FROM THE
I-SPY BOOK OF ANIMALS

Leucrocuta Donkey-sized, with one toothbone that extends around its entire mouth. Best approached from behind, as it cannot turn its neck. Excellent mimic. Young naturalists are often lulled into calling out their name, then hearing it called back in their own voice, before being eaten. Score: 15 pts

ANIMAL CRACKERS

In August 2003, Benny Zavala of California was jailed for 50 days for murdering a government spy. To be more specific, he *thought* he was murdering a government spy. It was actually his daughter's pet guinea pig.

He had thought the pet's teeth were bar-coded and that there was a camera implanted in its head. The subsequent trial for cruelty to animals revealed that Zavala's excessive methamphetamine addiction may have had something to do with the illusion. 'It's not often you have someone this paranoid from using drugs that they think a guinea pig is spying on them for the government,' summed up Deputy District Attorney Tom Connors. Wise words indeed.

10 SONGS THAT WERE
ORIGINALLY ABOUT FISH

I Have a Bream	ABBA
Blenny Lane	The Beatles
Super Grouper	ABBA again
I'm a Sole Man	James Brown
Sprat outta Hell	Meatloaf
Herring my car	Gary Numan
Guppy Love	Donny Osmond
I Cod You Babe	Sonny Anchovy
I'll be Dogfish	Marlin Gaye
We gotta get troutta this plaice	The Animals

DEFYING GRAVITY

The treecreeper is a mouse-like bird that hops its way up the trunks and branches of trees using its long curved bill to pick out insects and larvae from its bark. It's a delightful sight as it hops in a spiral, investigating as it goes, before flying off to try another tree. Then as you're watching it hop along the underside of the branch, you suddenly wonder – why doesn't it fall off? The answer is that as it makes each jump upside-down, it briefly flaps its wings, propelling itself back up to the branch again, although the movement is almost imperceptible to the human eye.

QUOTE UNQUOTE

It's better to feed one cat than many birds.
Scandinavian proverb

FROGS ARE FUNNY

A man walks into the doctor's with a frog attached to his head.
'Good Lord,' says the doctor. 'How on earth did you get this
awful condition?'
'No idea, doc,' says the frog. 'It started as a
wart on my bottom.'

LUCK IN BLACK AND WHITE

One for sorrow
Two for joy
Three for a girl
Four for a boy
Five for silver
Six for gold
Seven for a secret never to be told
Eight for Heaven
Nine for Hell
Ten and you'll meet the Devil himself

This counting rhyme of magpies dates from the belief that members of the crow family brought luck in varying degrees, probably due to their generally black plumage. The disappearance of ravens from the Tower of London, the appearance of a crow on the roof of your house, the sight of crows nesting together, are all apparent signs of impending doom.

The fact that different numbers of magpies can bring alternative results in your life (three means the birth of a girl, four a boy, for example), is likely because of their pied colouring, a roughly even mixture of black and white. Many people today still blink when they see one bird, to turn that single bird into two sightings and bring joy.

Today, magpies have become increasingly common birds in town and countryside. Looks as if we'll all be meeting up with the Devil, then.

OUT WITH GOUT

Meadow saffron is one of the oldest medicinal plants still in pharmaceutical use today. Its ability to help treat joint pains was recorded as far back as 100 AD, and today its active alkaloid constituent is recognised as a valuable drug, colchicine, for the treatment of acute gout.

SITES FOR SORE EYES

There's history aplenty at St Catherine's Hill, the nature reserve near Winchester run by the Hampshire and Isle of Wight Wildlife Trust. It starts with bronze age pits, continues with iron age ramparts, encompasses Saxon boundaries, and is the site of the Norman chapel that gives the hill its name. Moving to medieval times, look out for the dry valleys known as dongas, ancient trackways that were originally worn away by animal-drawn carts. Up to the 17th century, now, and the 'mizmaze' still stands as a fun feature for children to run around. Even the 20th century has its moment: the site was made famous in the 1990s as the setting for the Twyford Down/M3 protests.

But history isn't all the reserve has to offer: natural history is in abundance, too. Over 350 species of flora adorn this hilly stretch of unimproved chalk downland, including several species of orchid. Look out for the well disguised green hairstreak, while the brown argus, chalkhill and small blue are also among the butterfly contingent. The clumps of beech woodland are home to devil's bolete, while winter brings flocks of fieldfare and redwing.

CRYPTIC CREATURES AND PUZZLING PLANTS

Take the first letter from a British mammal to leave a beast of burden.
Answer on page 153

SO GOOD THEY NAMED IT TWICE

Creatures with scientific generic and specific names that match (tautonyms) include:

Grass snake	*Natrix natrix*
Sole	*Solea solea*
Edible dormouse	*Glis glis*
Otter	*Lutra lutra*
Badger	*Meles meles*
Greylag goose	*Anser anser*
Grey Partridge	*Perdix perdix*
Black-tailed godwit	*Limosa limosa*
Wren	*Troglodytes troglodytes*
Sallow kitten moth	*Furcula furcula*

QUOTE UNQUOTE

I believe in God, only I spell it Nature.
FRANK LLOYD WRIGHT, architect

MEANWHILE, IN A FOREIGN LAND...

The honeycreepers of Hawaii are a complex and versatile group of birds, yet many are severely endangered, the introduction of rats and cats to the island, along with deforestation and the rapid spread of disease already bringing many of the species to extinction. Much work is being done to save those on the brink, with hope that some of the most exotically named creatures may yet struggle through another century. Apart from the conservation issues, there is the matter of some of the most beautiful names in the bird world.

How could we lose the:

Akiapola'au

Akikiki

Maui Alauahio

Anianiou

Oahu Amakihi

O'u

Nukupu'u

I'iwi

Akohekohe

Very little hope remains for the Po'o-uli, however. Only two females and one male remain.

HOW ENDEERING

Red deer are among nature's greatest recyclers. There are few waste materials that they do not put to good use.

For a start, there's the velvet. This is a blood-rich skin that encourages summer antler-growth. Once the antler has grown, the velvet rubs off, revealing the sturdy antlers within. Rather than litter the countryside, the stag often eats the discarded velvet for nutrients.

The following spring, the dead antler bones drop off, velvet reforms over the stub, and the process begins anew. In the peat-filled Scottish Highlands, stags gain extra nutrients such as calcium and phosphorous from chewing their discarded antlers.

Birthing of young calves begins in late May and continues through to late July, with the majority of calves being born in early to mid-June. After the placenta has been expelled, the hind will eat it and clean any traces of the birth from the area, to minimise the risk of attracting predators.

Still mindful of these predators while suckling her calf, the hind will eat its faeces and urine, to reduce the scent of young deer in the area. This is the most dangerous time: 80% of calf deaths take place in the week after birth.

The insect was flying rather slowly by me over the heath – a thin, yellow-bodied, long-legged creature, a *Tipula*, about half as big as our familiar crane-fly. Now, as flew by me about on a level with my thighs, up from the heath at my feet shot out a second insect, about the same size as the first, also a *Dipteron*, but of another family – one of the *Asilidae*, which are rapacious. The *Asilus* was also very long-legged, and seizing the other with its legs, the two fell together to the ground. Stooping down, I witnessed the struggle. The were locked together, and I saw the attacking insect raise his head and the forepart of his body so as to strike, then plunge his rostrum like a dagger in the soft part of his victim's body. Again and again he raised and buried his weapon in the other, and the other still refused to die or to cease struggling. And this little fight and struggle of two flies curiously moved me, and for some time I could not get over the feeling of intense repugnance it excited. This feeling was wholly due to association: the dagger-like weapon and the action of the insect were curiously human-like, and I had seen just such a combat between two men, one fallen and the other on him, raising and striking down with his knife. Had I never witnessed such an incident, the two flies struggling, one killing the other, would have produced no such feeling, and would not have been remembered.

WH Hudson, *Hampshire Days*

NOT JUST FOR BEETLING ABOUT

There's something about owning a car named after an animal that gets drivers all het up and excitable, particularly in America. Or so it would seem from the number of such vehicles that get churned off the production lines. Here's a list of cars that apparently had a certain type of animalistic driver in mind. Although it makes you wonder about the folk that chose the VW Rabbit.

AC Cobra
Buick Wildcat
Chevrolet Corvette Stingray
Chevrolet Impala
Dodge Ram
Dodge Viper
Ford Mustang
Jaguar
Mercury Cougar
Mercury Lynx
Mercury Sable
Triumph Stag
VW Rabbit
...and Panda car

DOES WHATEVER A SPIDER CAN

Perhaps it's because his powers are based on an animal himself, but Spider-Man has more than his fair share of creature-based foes. Here's a sample of villains who've been put on ice by the friendly neighbourhood Spider-Man over the last 40 years. (He's also gone toe to toe with Kraven the Hunter, although any hunter who goes around with that moniker sounds, frankly, pretty easy to beat)

Vulture ....Bald and can fly
Rhino ....Huge, with a horn and super-hard skinsuit
Kangaroo ....Leaps about a lot
Gibbon ....Swings about a lot
Scorpion...Watch the sting in the tail
Doctor Octopus ....Cybernetic arms with pincers in the ends
Lizard ....Ferocious and reptilian
Hammerhead...................Mafia boss with a flat, ramming head
Puma ....Careful of those claws
Tarantula...Poisoned tips to his shoes
Beetle ....Little more than a flying thief
Chameleon..Master of disguise
Eel ....Slippery customer
Grizzly ....Big, bad and hairy
Human Fly..Climbs walls. Scary

THE MAGAZINE OF CHOICE

With the exception of membership magazines that are put together by wildlife charities, such as The Wildlife Trusts' own *Natural World*, the general public interested in nature is poorly served by Britain's publishing industry. In amongst the copious newsstand publications on cookery, gardening, cars, dvds and even body-building, barely two or three wildlife magazines can be found.

There is, however, a magazine that everyone interested in natural history should subscribe to. *British Wildlife Magazine*, published by British Wildlife Publishing, has been sent to subscribers six times annually for the last 15 years. It carries excellent information on all aspects of British nature, from conservation news to regional environmental programmes, species accounts to historical and social studies. Its columnists include Peter Marren and Robert Burton, and every issue carries a round-up of seasonal wildlife sightings for the previous two months. For more information on this highly recommended magazine for the modern naturalist, call 01256 760663, or visit www.britishwildlife.co.uk.

SITES FOR SORE EYES

If you're a jaded city liver who wants to hear birds singing; if you need inspiration to make your garden work for wildlife; if you've never been to Frog Day; if you would like reassurance that wildlife gardening and city nature conservation can be a giggle, then London's Centre for Wildlife Gardening is the place to visit. Run by the London Wildlife Trust, it contains wild ponds, mini-meadows, hedges, and the cutest little birch woodland, all designed to display the urban heritage of back-yard diversity.

Its information centre is insulated with recycled newspaper pulp, and designed to catch the sun, hold the heat and stay cool in summer. Children can discover wildlife crafts, go on minibeast hunts, learn compost-making and pond-dipping skills and join the summer Eco-Club. Adults, meanwhile, can learn more about how best to garden for wildlife at home.

CRYPTIC CREATURES AND PUZZLING PLANTS

Which of the following is not an African antelope:
Suni, Bongo, Nyala, Zorilla, Oribi, Tsessebe?
Answer on page 153

NATURE NOTES

It is pleasant to observe any growth in a wood. There is the tract north-east of Beck Stow's Swamp, where some years since I used to go a-blackberrying and observed that the pitch pines were beginning to come in; and I have frequently noticed since how fairly they grew, clothing the plain as evenly as if dispersed by art. At first the young pines lined each side of the path like a palisade, they grew so densely, crowding each other to death in this wide world. Eleven years ago I was first aware that I walked in a pitch-pine wood there, and not a blackberry field – which erelong, perchance, I shall survey and lot off for a wood auction, and see the choppers at their work. These trees, I said to myself, are destined for the locomotive's maw; but fortunately it has changed its diet of late, and their branches, which it has taken so many years to mature, are regarded even by the woodman as trash.

Henry David Thoreau, *Faith in a Seed*

QUOTE UNQUOTE

*I am not a vegetarian because I love animals; I am a vegetarian
because I hate plants.*
A WHITNEY BROWN, US comedian

MEANWHILE, IN A FOREIGN LAND...

The island of New Guinea, second largest in the world, is home to many unusual creatures, but few can match the singing dog. Similar to the dingo, the New Guinea singing dog has a synchronised howl, in which different tones blend with each other. To hear it is an eerie experience. Their bodies are just as flexible as their voices: they can squeeze through any opening large enough to admit their head.

Singing dogs are feral, descended from dogs brought to the island along with human migrations many thousands of years ago. They moved to the mountains, where they developed thicker, slightly longer coats than other wild dogs. In 1948, a pair were captured and brought to Sydney Zoo in Australia, where the breed became internationally famous, and by the 1960s, singing dogs, despite their feral nature, were in high demand across Europe. Today, the breed is endangered in New Guinea, and possibly even extinct, yet in captivity it is still made to sing for its supper. Two individuals even once accompanied opera star Benita Valente on television.

HUNT DOWN YOUR QUARRY

There's an intriguing relationship between conservation groups, such as The Wildlife Trusts, and quarrying companies that extract sand and gravel from the land. The gravel pits that result, as water fills the quarried areas, can turn into some of the best and richest wildlife sites in the country.

Sites such as Lackford Lakes in Suffolk and Attenborough in Nottinghamshire represent how borrowed land can be returned with interest, as they now provide a wide range of habitats for birds, plants, insects and mammals. Summer dragonflies and winter wildfowl gatherings are often a major feature of gravel pits, while at Lackford, for example, rarities such as Caspian tern and spoonbill may well turn up during the migration seasons.

HERE COMES THE SUN

The changing wildlife patterns and early springs created by global warming are unlikely to abate. According to the Met Office, 2003 was officially the sunniest year ever recorded in both England and Scotland.

In England, 1,776.7 hours of sunshine were recorded, beating the previous sunniest in 1995 with 1,729.7 recorded hours. Meanwhile in Scotland, 1,386.6 hours were recorded, again beating 1995 which had 1,381.3 hours. Scotland also had its warmest year with an average temperature of 8.26°C (previous highest 8.07°C in 1997).

CATCH THE MOUSE

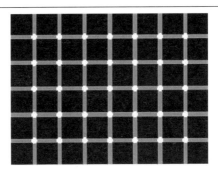

The black dots are mice running around a maze.
To catch one, all you have to do is stare at it.

LIKING LICHENS

Lichen conservation and monitoring is rarely reported in the press. Yet the importance of study of these composite plant organisms cannot be underestimated. Lichens are not single organisms, but symbiotic associations between plant and fungus that grow very slowly, and are generally dependent upon unpolluted habitat. Extremely sensitive to light conditions, moisture and temperature, they are hard to relocate, but with care and attention, they can be grown in gardens. The British Lichen Society, in fact, recommends that extra inducements to growth can be introduced; in other words, if you're trying to get some lichens growing in your rock garden, try coaxing them in with coatings of beer, yogurt, skimmed milk or even porridge.

Some species have got intriguing names: White script, goblin lights, arctic kidney, alpine sulphur-tresses and river jelly-lichen being among their number. The latter is now virtually extinct in mainland Europe, but still thrives in several of Scotland's finest salmon rivers.

But beware: lichenology can become a fixating subject. The story was told in 1999 of a woman driver who pulled out of a car park, only to notice that she was being followed. After a while she began to get nervous, and tried to lose her pursuer, but with no success. Deciding to confront the situation, she pulled her Lada over, and the car behind pulled up. A man got out and approached her. 'Sorry to disturb you,' he said, peering over her shoulder, 'but I noticed you had a rare species of lichen growing at the base of your car window. Mind if I take a closer look?'

LADYBIRD, LADYBIRD...

When an insect closes its wings behind its back, they automatically fold in a particular pattern, rather as when you close an umbrella, and the spokes inside collapse in on themselves, (although in the case of insect wings the role of the spokes is played by veins). Yet ladybirds, as do some other insects, have wings that naturally extend beyond their wingcases, or elytra, and need to be drawn in. How do they achieve this, particularly as they have no muscles in the wings themselves?

Next time you see a ladybird land, watch carefully. The wings get pulled underneath the elytra fairly slowly. This is because the ladybird is raising its abdomen so that tiny bristles attach themselves near the base of the wings, then pulling its abdomen forward, dragging the wings with it. It drops the abdomen again, stretches it back, engages with the next section of wing, and drags that in too, until the wings are neatly tucked away.

MEANWHILE, IN A FOREIGN LAND...

When Madagascar split away from Africa 165 million years ago, its flora and fauna evolved quite independently from that of the mainland. Lemurs are the best known example of creatures that are endemic to the island, but the largest lemur of all is the most extraordinary. The indri, reasonably common until a century ago, but now numbering only a few thousand individuals, weighs up to 22lb and only comes down to the ground to cross treeless areas, or sometimes to eat dirt. Giving birth only once every two or three years, the indri emits an eerie call that sounds human in tone, and is picked up by other indri through the rainforest, surrounding the listener with wailing, child-like howls. Unsurprisingly, many legends exist in Madagascar relating to indris giving birth to human children.

Incidentally, the animal gets its name from the Malagasy for 'Look at that', which is what the first arriving Europeans were told when the lemur was pointed out to them.

QUOTE UNQUOTE

A hippo does not have a sting in its tail, but a wise man would still rather be sat on by a bee.
POLISH PROVERB

As one might expect, the authors of the New Naturalist series come from a wide variety of backgrounds and vary enormously in terms of personality, outlook and career. The one thing they have in common, of course, is that they wrote a book for our series. In doing so, and bearing in mind that the majority of them were asked to do so, they were expressing no superficial aspect of their outlook. Reading about them – and by the nature of things, more is available about the dead than the living – it is clear that natural history meant a great deal to these people. In many cases, it lay at the root of things, whether they became professional biologists or remained as gifted amateurs. The were 'new' naturalists in the 1940s sense of embracing the recent advances of science to illuminate the workings of nature; but in another sense their approach was rather old-fashioned. Their contributions to science, though considerable, were almost entirely non-technological. Nearly all of these authors were first and foremost masters of field study, based on observation and simple experiment. They were not so much interested in data sets and theoretical modelling as in the relationships and behaviours or living wild animals and plants, or with the shaping of the scenery. The other matter that we can usefully notice at the start, because it is less common among scientists today, is that they were good communicators and could write in plain, everyday language without over-simplifying; and in some cases, they wrote extraordinarily well.

Peter Marren, *The New Naturalists*
The book was published in 1995 to celebrate 50 years of the Collins
New Naturalist imprint. It was, itself, number 82 in the series

GONE DOWN IN NATURAL HISTORY

Wildlife named after musicians

Mozartella beethoveni – a wasp.
Fernandocrambus chopinellus – a moth.
Funkotriplogynium iagobadius – a mite. *Iago Badius* is Latin for
James Brown. *Funko*– needs no explanation.
Mackenziurus johnnyi, M. joeyi, M. deedeei, M. ceejayi – trilobites.
Named after the Ramones.
Greeffiella beatlei – a nematode worm with a shaggy mane.
Masiakasaurus knopfleri – a dinosaur. The fossil-hunters noticed
that they tended to have more success when they played Dire Straits.
Knopfler said later: 'the fact that it's a dinosaur is certainly apt'.
Aegrotocatellus jaggeri – a trilobite.
Arcticalymene viciousi, A. rotteni, A. jonesi, A. cooki, A. matlocki –
trilobites. Named after the Sex Pistols.
Hyla stingi – a Columbian tree frog. Named after the singer for his
work in rainforest conservation.

6 ONOMATOPOEIC BRITISH BIRDS

Cuckoo
Chiffchaff
Hoopoe
Pipit
Curlew
Turtle dove

YOU'RE SURE OF A BIG SURPRISE

There's something of the Merrie Olde England about the wild boar…
but increasingly there may something of the Merrie New England, too.
Reports suggest that there could be as many as 1,000 of them wandering and snuffling around the woodlands of south-east England, the offspring of escapees from boar farms that have been husbanding the animal for meat since the early 1980s.

Boar are controversial animals. Weighing up to 400lb, tusked, and faster than the fastest man, they are seen by many to be dangerous creatures if disturbed. Farmers, too, worry that the animals may be powerful enough to break into their fields. Yet wild boars are also wonders for the habitat, their rooting creating shallows, rough areas and extra soil fertility that are ideal for plant growth, while invasive rhododendron populations fall before their snouts.

Should the wild boar be allowed to live in Britain outside of captivity?
The jury is still out.

THE NATURE GUIDE

In 2004, Sir David Attenborough celebrates 50 years of broadcasting natural history programmes. His are the voice and the enthusiasm that have for years introduced countless Britons to the wonders of the natural world. For many readers of this book, Sir David is the ultimate Wildlife Companion. His televisual history includes:

1954-1964	Zoo Quest	1993	Wildlife 10
1975	The Explorers	1993	Life in the Freezer
1976	The Tribal Eye	1995	The Private Life of Plants
1977	Wildlife on One	1996	Attenborough in
1979	Life on Earth		Paradise
1984	The Living Planet	1997	The Wildlife Specials
1987	The First Eden	1998	The Life of Birds
1989	Lost Worlds,	2000	State of the Planet
	Vanished Lives	2001	The Blue Planet
1990	The Trials of Life	2002	The Life of Mammals

NATURE TREK

A useful glossary for when you're discussing wildlife with a Klingon:
bo'Degh – bird, the most general word for a bird-like creature
cha'bIp – a bird noted for its speed
cha'qu' – a bird with a noisy, repetitive cry
ghotI' – fish, most general word for fish-like creature
jajlo' Qa' – a noisy animal (not a bird) known for making a
ruckus at dawn, like a rooster
lIr – a nocturnal bird
lotlhmoq – a bird that swoops into the water in order to
catch food, but cannot swim
naHjej – thistle
neb – beak, bill
notqa' – a large, black bird (although nowhere near as large as a
qa'rol, which is really big)
qanraD – a bird known for its song
qaryoq – bird capable of mimicking speech
Qaj – type of animal with brown lips
Qa'Hom – an animal (not a bird), like a Qa' but smaller
raw' – an aquatic bird with colorful plumage
tangqa' – animal species with both genders resembling a bull
toQ – a bird of prey
vem'eq – a bird that feeds almost exclusively on the serpent worm
from which *qagh* is made. (Please note that Klingons are not
particularly fond of this bird.)
waqboch – a bird with a very long beak
And for the real experts among you:
cha'Do' – a species of Klingon bird about which little is known

TO TICK OR NOT TO TICK

Sometimes, twitchers – the Martinis of the birding world ('Anytime, any place, anywhere') – find themselves in something of a dilemma. Part of the point of twitching is to tick off as many rare birds as possible, so a British first is a must-see. When, in October 1998, news came through that a grey catbird had shown up in Southampton, the twitching world was abuzz. Never had this bird been seen in Britain before. The only problem was, it had come across on a cruise liner, and remained on board the whole time the ship was docked at port.

The agony was rife. Would it be possible to see this mega-tick? Could the ship be boarded? And would it count anyway, as the bird had clearly had some assistance in its trip across the Atlantic. Consciences had plenty to wrestle with. Finally, the liner left port for the Mediterranean, and the catbird finally jumped ship at Malta. All's well that ends well. Another catbird turned up at Anglesey in October 2001, and the species finally joined the British list. Relief all round.

The myths told by native Americans are among the strongest examples of belief in the importance of understanding nature. White Buffalo Woman is a central myth of the Lakota, or Sioux. It tells how the Lakota first received their sacred pipe and the ceremony in which to use it. To the Lakota this is probably the most important of all their myths.

In the days before the Lakota had horses on which to hunt the buffalo, food was often scarce. One summer when the Lakota nation had camped together, there was very little to eat. Two young men of the Itazipcho band – the 'Without-Bows' – decided they would rise early and look for game. They left the camp while the dogs were still yawning, and set out across the plain, accompanied only by the song of the yellow meadowlark.

After a while the day began to grow warm. Crickets chirruped in the waving grass, prairie dogs darted into their holes as the braves approached, but still there was no real game. So the young men made towards a little hill from which they would see further across the vast expanse of level prairie. Reaching it, they shielded their eyes and scanned the distance, but what they saw coming out of the growing heat haze was something bright, that seemed to go on two legs, not four. In a while they could see that it was a very beautiful woman in shining white buckskin.

As the woman came closer, they could see that her buckskin was wonderfully decorated with sacred designs in rainbow-coloured porcupine quills. She carried a bundle on her back, and a fan of fragrant sage leaves in her hand. Her jet-black hair was loose, except for a single strand tied with buffalo fur. Her eyes were full of light and power, and the young men were transfixed.

Now one of the men was filled with a burning desire. 'What a woman!' he said sideways to his friend. 'And all alone on the prairie. I'm going to make the most of this!'

'You fool,' said the other. 'This woman is holy.'

But the foolish one had made up his mind, and when the woman beckoned him towards her, he needed no second invitation. As he reached out for her, they were both enveloped in a great cloud. When it lifted, the woman stood there, while at her feet was nothing but a pile of bones with terrible snakes writhing among them.

'Behold,' said the woman to the good brave. 'I am coming to your people with a message from Tatanka Oyate, the buffalo nation. Return to Chief Standing Hollow Horn and tell him what you have seen. Tell him to prepare a tipi large enough for all his people, and to get ready for my coming.'

The young man ran back across the prairie and was gasping for breath as he reached his camp. With a small crowd of people already following him, he found

Standing Hollow Horn and told him what had happened, and that the woman was coming. The chief ordered several tipis to be combined into one big enough for his band. The people waited excitedly for the woman to arrive. After four days the scouts posted to watch for the holy woman saw something coming towards them in a beautiful manner from across the prairie. Then suddenly the woman was in the great lodge, walking round it in a sunwise direction. She stopped before Standing Hollow Horn in the west of the lodge, and held her bundle before him in both hands. 'Look on this,' she said, 'and always love and respect it. No one who is impure should ever touch this bundle, for it contains the sacred pipe.'

She unrolled the skin bundle and took out a pipe, and a small round stone which she put down on the ground.

'With this pipe you will walk on the earth, which is your grandmother and your mother. The earth is sacred, and so is every step that you take on her. The bowl of the pipe is of red stone; it is the earth. Carved into it and facing the centre is the buffalo calf, who stands for all the four-leggeds. The stem is of wood, which stands for all that grows on the earth. These twelve hanging feathers from the Spotted Eagle stand for all the winged creatures. All these living things of the universe are the children of Mother Earth. You are all joined as one family, and you will be reminded of this when you smoke the pipe. Treat this pipe and the earth with respect, and your people will increase and prosper.'

The woman told them that seven circles carved on the stone represented the seven rites in which the people would learn to use the sacred pipe. The first was for the rite of 'keeping the soul', which she now taught them. The remaining rites they would learn in due course.

The woman made as if to leave the lodge, but then she turned and spoke to Standing Hollow Horn again. 'This pipe will carry you to the end. Remember that in me there are four ages. I am going now, but I will look on your people in every age, and at the end I will return.'

She now walked slowly around the lodge in a sunwise direction. The people were silent and filled with awe. Even the hungry young children watched her, their eyes alive with wonder. Then she left. But after she had walked a short distance, she faced the people again and sat down on the prairie. The people gazing after her were amazed to see that when she stood up she had become a young red and brown buffalo calf. The calf walked further into the prairie, and then lay down and rolled over, looking back at the people.

When she stood up she was a white buffalo. The white buffalo walked on until she was a bright speck in the distant prairie, and then rolled over again, and became a black buffalo. This buffalo walked away, stopped, bowed to the four directions of the earth, and finally disappeared over the hill.

SPOT THE DOG

He's in there somewhere.

MEANWHILE, IN A FOREIGN LAND...

The higher you pee, the greater your power. This seems to be the message put out by the giant pandas of China who adopt an intriguing range of positions in order to deposit their scent. In addition to the usual squatting approach, they have been seen cocking one leg, backing up against walls or trees, and even doing handstands as they relieve themselves. It's only the adult males who perform the handstand, and sub-adult males, when sniffing other panda urine, tend to back further away from the higher scent deposits.

Presumably, scent height is an indicator of athletic ability rather than size (unless the younger pandas are fooled into thinking that there are some 20ft individuals out there), and thus competitive advantage. A true case of not wanting to be a little squirt.

CRYPTIC CREATURES AND PUZZLING PLANTS

Which of the following is not a moth:
Lettuce shark,
Great leopard,
Isabelline tiger,
Waved tabby,
Rusty-spotted cat?
Answer on page 153

SITES FOR SORE EYES

Wordsworth and Coleridge were inspired by the Falls of Clyde in Lanarkshire, as have been dozens of artists through the years. Now that the site is run by the Scottish Wildlife Trust, this dramatic tumble of water with its surrounding riverside habitat can continue to inspire in the decades ahead. Peregrine, otter, dipper and badger all make their home near the river – and the views of the peregrines in particular are exceptional.

Scotland's first public hydro-electric scheme was opened here in 1927, joined in more recent years by a wildlife centre. Yet the wildlife itself is what makes the reserve truly breath-taking: five species of bat fly overhead on summer evening strolls; campion, water avens and marsh marigolds adorn the riverside trail. A rich mosaic of fungi is a feature of the autumn months, while secretive roe deer are never far away. Visit in the evenings for accompanied badger-watching.

A WILDLIFE RAINBOW

Red fox
Orange footman
Yellow wagtail
Green tiger beetle
Bluebottle
Indigo bush
Violet

FROGS ARE FUNNY

Two frogs are sitting on a lilypad having a chat. 'You know what happened to me today?' says one. 'I was sitting on the bank, just minding my own business, when I yawned, and a tasty bluebottle flew right into my mouth.'
'That's great,' says the other. 'But I was even luckier. I was sitting on the other bank, watching a couple of flies way above my head, when they bumped into each other and landed right at my feet.'
An otter swims past. 'Couldn't help overhearing you guys,' it says. 'But I can top that. I was just lounging around on the far bank this morning, when a fish leapt out of the water, cannoned off a passing blackbird, bounced off a duck's back, and landed right in front of me.'
'That's extraordinary', says the first frog to the second. 'I didn't know otters could talk.'

TIPS FOR IN-CAR RELAXATION

As recommended by Kwik-fit fitters everywhere

Juniper helps breathing and concentration.
Mint assists breathing and calm.
Seaweed stimulates mental activity and is recommended in moments of confusion and anger.
Camomile has calming properties for nervousness.
Fern is a plant with a delicate aroma and relaxing qualities.
Freesia is known for its anti-depressant and relaxing qualities.
Grapefruit restores health and enthusiasm and is used to combat difficult moments.

GONE DOWN IN NATURAL HISTORY

Wildlife named after actors and film-makers

Attenborosaurus – a plesiosaur. Named after David, the naturalist, not Richard, the Jurassic Park actor.

Calponia harrisonfordi – a spider. For his work in documentary narration. At least it wasn't a snake.

Norasaphus monroeae – a trilobite. The fossil has a curvy hourglass shape.

Orsonwelles othello, O. macbeth, O. falstaffius, O. ambersonorum – giant Hawaiian spiders

Rostropria garbo – a wasp. The female of the species is solitary.

Utahraptor spielbergi – a dinosaur. Discovered mere days before the premiere of *Jurassic Park*, this raptor, larger than any found before, showed that Spielberg's filmic beasts, derided for their large size, were possible after all. An extraordinary case of nature coming to the PR rescue of a film-maker. The dinosaur's name, incidentally, was not registered properly, and is now *U. ostrommaysorum*.

ITSY BITSY FEAR

I have fought a grizzly bear
Tracked a cobra to its lair
Killed a crocodile who dared to cross my path
But the thing I really dread
When I've just got out of bed
Is to find that there's a spider in the bath.
MICHAEL FLANDERS and DONALD SWANN, *The Spider*

WHAT MAKES THE WILDCAT WILD?

The Scottish wildcat is one of Britain's rarest and most elusive mammals. Its future, however, remains uncertain for many reasons. Habitat loss and persecution are among them, but hybridising with feral domestic cats is also slowly diluting the animal's pure stock. How, then, could you identify a wildcat as being a genuine *Felis silvestris* and not a *Felis catus* hybrid?

Look at the four stripes on the nape.
They should be wavy and broad.

The dorsal stripe should end at the tail root.

The feet have no white patches.

The rump has no spots on it.

The bushy tail is short with a black tip.

THE SOUND OF SUMMER HOLIDAYS

Cicadas are associated with holidays in warmer climes, calling constantly from some nearby perch as you sip your sundowner and stare out into the dusk from your white-washed villa.

Yet you don't have to go as far as the Mediterranean to find cicadas – we've got a species of our own in Britain.

The New Forest cicada is only found in the eponymous area, and its high-pitched song is rarely heard, but it's here nonetheless. First recorded in Britain in 1812, it used to have strongholds in Surrey, but has been confined to the New Forest since the early 20th century. Assumed to be extinct in this country for 25 years, it was rediscovered in 1962, where it holds on in about 26 sites in the Forest.

If you want to hear a cicada, this is what you should listen for, according to specialists Bryan Pinchen and Lena Ward: 'The locating song has one or two short warming-up chirrups of two to three seconds and is separated from the courtship song by a variable length of time. Courtship song can last several minutes, and is produced at a low amplitude before rising progressively to a higher volume, from which it sinks a little in the last few seconds before halting. It is best described as a faint, high-pitched ringing buzz, inaudible to most people over the age of 40, but younger people with good hearing can detect it over distances of 60m or more.'

So if you've got good hearing and you're planning a trip to the New Forest… don't forget the sundowner.

NATURE NOTES

Birds are everywhere and, while you may not notice it, I do. So do all birders. Like them, I identify or, at least, attempt to identify every single one I see, without exception. I look at birds as I walk for the morning milk, when I go to the postbox, as I drive the car. I've recorded birds in the middle of the night, waking up to hear migrants flying above the house. On the day my second daughter was born I noted a flock of wild swans passing over at three in the morning. Friends have seen good birds while waiting to be served at the cheese counter in a supermarket. People birdwatch from their office. I have a pair of binoculars on my desk here, now, as I write, just in case.

Mark Cocker, *Birders: Tales of a Tribe*

FICTIONAL TALES THAT COULD HAVE BEEN A BIT MORE EQUINE

The Mare of Casterbridge
Tis Pity She's a Horse
The Bridle of Dracula
Ass You Like It
Donkey Ote
The BFGG
And one that couldn't: Equus

THE LITTLE GENTLEMAN

In 1702, King William III, otherwise known as William of Orange, was riding his horse around Hampton Court. Sorrel – for that was the horse's name, tripped on a molehill, throwing the king to the ground. He died three weeks later 'from the complications of a fractured clavicle; he developed pneumonia, which complicated his pre-existing heart trouble, and probably suffered a terminal pulmonary embolism' (Clifford Brewer, *The Death of Kings*). The Jacobites, followers of King James II, who had had their position of power usurped by the Protestant William, were delighted. It is said that they raised a toast to the 'little gentleman in black velvet' who had given brief hope to their exiled king.

QUOTE UNQUOTE

When one tugs at a single thing in nature, he finds it attached to the rest of the world.
JOHN MUIR, naturalist

NATURE NOTES

The wise man will never weary of looking at green grass and green trees. It is an unspeakable refreshment to the eye and the mind: and the daily pressure of occupation cannot touch one here. One wonders that human beings who always live amid such scenery do not look more like it. But some people are utterly unimpressionable by the influences of outward scenery. You may know men who have lived for many years where Nature has done her best with wood and rock and river: and even when you become well acquainted with the, you cannot discover the faintest trace in their talk or in their feeling of the mightily powerful touch (as it would be to so many) which has been unceasingly laid upon them through all that time. Or you may have beheld a vacuous person at a picnic party, who amid traces of God's handiwork that should make men hold their breath, does but pass from the occupation of fatuously flirting with a young woman like himself, to furiously abusing the servants for not sufficiently cooling the wine... A human being ought to be very thankful if his disposition be such that he heartily enjoys green grass and green trees.

Autumn Holidays of a Country Parson, 1865
(Author known as 'A.K.H.B.')

SPORTING FLIGHTS OF FANCY

Birdie – a cute little flying creature, or one shot under par in golf
Eagle – a rather larger flying creature, or two shots under par in golf
Albatross – an extremely large flying creature, or three shots under par in golf
Feather – an item for aiding flying creatures, or a boxing weight for small people
Bantam – a creature that can barely fly, or a boxing weight for smaller people
Fly – a tiny flying creature, or a boxing weight for very small people
Bat – a nocturnal flying creature, or a hunk of willow for despatching trundlers in cricket
Duck – a flying creature, or a cricketing occasion when the trundler rapidly gets the better of the hunk of willow

QUOTE UNQUOTE

Animals have these advantages over man: they never hear the clock strike, they die without any idea of death, they have no theologians to instruct them, their last moments are not disturbed by unwelcome and unpleasant ceremonies, their funerals cost them nothing, and no one starts lawsuits over their wills.
VOLTAIRE, writer and philosopher

Bird ringing for scientific purposes as we know it today began in Denmark in 1899, but there are much earlier examples of methods of marking particular individuals, as these swallow tales show:

During the Punic wars in the 3rd century BC, nesting swallows were smuggled out of one besieged Ligurian garrison and taken to headquarters, behind the lines. They were then marked and set free, carrying messages back to the front.

A few centuries later, swallows were again used, but this time in betting scams. Betting took place in various places around Italy on the chariot races in Rome, and bets were often still taken long after news of the result was announced in the provinces. Swallows would be taken from these outlying towns to Rome, and released with coloured threads indicating the winner tied to their legs.

In 1250, a German monk told of a swallow that had had a piece of parchment attached to its leg with the words 'Oh swallow, where do you live in winter' written upon it. The swallow allegedly returned the following year with a note that replied 'In Asia, in home of Petrus'.

ZOO QUESTION

When David Attenborough started planning *Zoo Quest* in 1954, he was looking for a peg to hang the programme on. Deciding that a search for rare animals around the world would be of interest to viewers, he set off to Sierra Leone in a hunt for the rare bald-headed rock crow, or *Picathartes gymnocephalus*. By the time the first episode aired, the *Zoo Quest* team was able to show film of an array of creatures, from chameleons to starlings, weaver birds to pythons, but no *Picathartes*. At the end of each episode, Attenborough would advise viewers to tune in next week to find out if the bird might appear.

After about four or five episodes, Attenborough was wondering whether the show was successful. Were people interested? One day, he was making his way down Regent Street in London, when a bus pulled up alongside him. The driver rolled down his window. 'Oy, Dave', he shouted, 'are you going to catch that *Picafartees gymno*-bloody-*cephalus* or aren't you?'

Soon afterwards, Attenborough confidently put in a successful bid for a second series. And yes, they did catch one.

Percentage decline of roost sizes of British bat between 1978 and 1992 73

WHICH MOUSE IN YOUR HOUSE?

House mice are probably the best known rodent co-inhabitants of our homes, yet the hibernating wood mice and yellow-necked mice are also reasonably common visitors, particularly in the southern counties. House mice are easy to identify – grey all over – but the two woodland species, which are darkish brown with white bellies, need a bit more work.

• The yellow-necked has a collar of yellow fur right across its neck, while the wood often has a yellow chest patch that doesn't join up with the brown fur on its back.

• The yellow-necked is a little larger and noisier than the wood, particularly when caught.

• Out of doors, the yellow-necked prefers mature deciduous woodland, while the wood is more flexible, found in hedgerows, arable fields and of course woodland.

OUR FEATHERED FRIENDS

Ross's gull
Rachel's malimbe
Say's phoebe
Ardea cinerea monicae – the Mauritanian heron
Acanthiza lineata chandleri – a subspecies of the striated thornbill
...and Joey, the baby kangaroo

MEANWHILE, IN A FOREIGN LAND

Until recently, little was known about life in tropical forest treetops, because getting up there was nearly impossible. Early explorers used ropes and pulleys or ladders carved into tree trunks. Today, biologists explore the canopy via towers, suspension bridges, rafts lowered gently onto treetops by dirigibles, and even construction cranes.

We now know that about 90% of all organisms in a rainforest are found in the canopy. The sun that barely reaches the forest floor strikes treetops with full force, fuelling the photosynthesis that results in leaves, fruit, and seeds. Since there's so much good food way up there, animals abound in the canopy.

For example, a study of rainforest canopy in Peru with 500 cubic metres of foliage (about the size of a two-car garage) found more than 50 species of ants, 1,000 beetle species, 1,700 arthropod species, and more than 100,000 individuals. A rainforest tree alone can have some 1,200 species of beetle, while a single hectare of rich forest canopy is projected to have 12,448 beetle species.

CRYPTIC CREATURES AND PUZZLING PLANTS

Change the bold letter in each word to make a new word, while
changing a language into an animal when the five new letters
are read downwards.

```
  |L|AME
M|A|LE
  |T|OLD
M|I|ND
  |N|IGHT
```

Answer on page 153

QUOTE UNQUOTE

*Animals generally return the love you lavish on them by a swift bite
in passing – not unlike friends and wives.*
GERALD DURRELL, naturalist and zoo-owner

A MILLENNIUM OF INTRODUCTIONS

As Britons colonised the world, so they brought back plants from
their travels that have in turn colonised this country. Some botanists,
such as Maggie Campbell-Culver, categorise the introduction of
plants in 10 phases, some of which overlap:

1000–1560 – plants arrive from continental Europe, due in part to
the Norman invasion and the Crusades.

1560–1620 – plants from the Near East, West Asia and the Balkans
began arriving.

1620–1662 – botanist John Tradescant brings plants from Russia and
the North African coast, and his son does the same from North
America.

1660–1720 – the introduction of shrubs and trees from the eastern
seaboard of North America.

1680–1774 – plant introductions from southern Africa, especially the
Cape of Good Hope.

1772–1820 – the Antipodean period, beginning with the return of
Joseph Banks and Captain Cook from the southern hemisphere.

1820–1860 – plants introduced from the west coast of North
America.

1840–1870 – plants come from South America.

1840–1890 – arrivals from expeditions to India and the Himalayas.

1890–1930 – plants arrive from China and Japan.

BIG FLEAS HAVE LITTLE FLEAS...

...Upon their backs to bite 'em
And little fleas have littler fleas
And so ad infinitum

Conopid flies have a Ridley Scottesque beginning: their pupae grow inside bees and wasps. The adults lay their eggs insect the insects by grappling with them in mid-air, and injecting the egg into the bee's abdominal cavity between its armoured body segments. Once the egg hatches, the maggot literally eats its way out.

But even these mini-beasts can be infested. A conopid maggot, already inside a bee, is sometimes got at by pteromalid wasps, which lay a tiny egg inside it (it's hard not to feel sorry for the poor beleaguered bee at this stage). As the maggot feeds on the bee, so the wasp egg, which hosts up to 40 wasps itself, develops. In spring, out comes the maggot, dying, from which out comes a host of wasps.

WHAT WAS THAT BIRD?

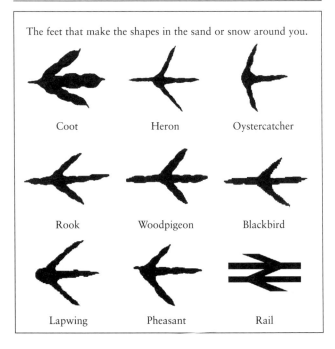

The feet that make the shapes in the sand or snow around you.

Coot

Heron

Oystercatcher

Rook

Woodpigeon

Blackbird

Lapwing

Pheasant

Rail

According to Herodotus, Aesop was a slave who lived in Samos in the 6th century BC and eventually was freed by his master. He also told some great tales.

The Vixen and the Lioness

A Vixen who was taking her babies out for an airing one balmy morning, came across a Lioness, with her cub in arms. 'Why such airs, haughty dame, over one solitary cub?' sneered the Vixen. 'Look at my healthy and numerous litter here, and imagine, if you are able, how a proud mother should feel.' The Lioness gave her a squelching look, and lifting up her nose, walked away, saying calmly, 'Yes, just look at that beautiful collection. What are they? Foxes! I've only one, but remember, that one is a Lion.'
Quality is better than quantity.

The Wolf and the Crane

A Wolf who had a bone stuck in his throat hired a Crane, for a large sum, to put her head into his mouth and draw out the bone. When the Crane had extracted the bone and demanded the promised payment, the Wolf, grinning and grinding his teeth, exclaimed: 'Why, you have surely already had a sufficient recompense, in having been permitted to draw out your head in safety from the mouth and jaws of a wolf.'
In serving the wicked, expect no reward, and be thankful if you escape injury for your pains.

The Lark and Her Young Ones

A Lark had made her nest in the early spring on the young green wheat. The brood had almost grown to their full strength and attained the use of their wings and the full plumage of their feathers, when the owner of the field, looking over his ripe crop, said, 'The time has come when I must ask all my neighbours to help me with my harvest.' One of the young Larks heard his speech and related it to his mother, inquiring of her to what place they should move for safety. 'There is no occasion to move yet, my son,' she replied; 'the man who only sends to his friends to help him with his harvest is not really in earnest.'

The owner of the field came again a few days later and saw the wheat shedding the grain from excess of ripeness. He said, 'I will come myself tomorrow with my labourers, and with as many reapers as I can hire, and will get in the harvest.' The Lark on hearing these words said to her brood, 'It is time now to be off, my little ones, for the man is in earnest this time; he no longer trusts his friends, but will reap the field himself.'
Self-help is the best help.

THE MARGARET THATCHER
OF THE BIRD WORLD

The nightjar is one of Britain's more enigmatic birds. Arriving from African in mid-May and returning in August, it emerges at dusk, flitting through the night hunting moths and other insects with its wide-open gape, then disappearing at dawn again as its mottled plumage blends perfectly with the lichen-covered logs and branches on which it roosts. It's night-time call is an eerie, vibrant churring song.

Unsurprisingly, then, the nightjar was a mysterious creature to earlier generations. Until the 17th century, it was still given the name goatsucker, as it was believed to feed on the milk of livestock. Indeed, even its scientific name – *Caprimulgus europaeus* – means 'European goat-milker'. For this reason, the bird was also called the Puck bird, or Puckeridge, after the impish spirit of the night Puck, who also was alleged to be a milk-snatcher.

A STOAT BY ANY OTHER NAME

Country names for the stoat

Carre
Clubster
Clubtail
Futteret
Lobster
Puttice
Whitterick
Whutherit

NATURE NOTES

Do you ever wonder if monkeys have a fear of falling? 30 metres up in the crown of a giant rainforest tree in Borneo, I was once observing young gibbons chasing each other in the branches. I was on an expedition surveying a largely unexplored part of Sarawak near Mount Mulu in northern Borneo. A female gibbon crashed into its brother, missed a handhold and spun out into the abyss, tumbling helplessly towards the forest floor. I was certain it would be injured, but it seemed totally unconcerned. Just above my head, the little female reached out and effortlessly grabbed a passing twig and, in one fluid movement, pulled itself into a tree before racing upwards to the canopy to join its family. It's millions of years since we humans used to be able to do that, and I thought, 'I wish I could do so now'.

Andrew Mitchell, *The Enchanted Canopy*

QUOTE UNQUOTE

The repetition in nature may not be a mere recurrence.
It may be a theatrical 'encore'.
GK CHESTERTON, writer

SITES FOR SORE EYES

Sandwich and Pegwell Bay, near Ramsgate, is one of the best complex habitats in the south-east. Blessed with intertidal mudflats, saltmarsh, shingle, sand dunes, ancient dune pasture, chalk cliffs and coastal scrubland, this Kent Wildlife Trust reserve is not only a wonderful place for birdwatchers, but is the perfect spot to see butterflies that have migrated from the continent. The reserve is of international importance for its wintering wildfowl, and during spring and autumn keep your neck craned for visiting migrants.

The site is botanically rich. Sea aster, sea lavender and the rare golden samphire can be found, while orchids are a delight. In addition to southern marsh and pyramidal, bee orchids are now flourishing under a scrub management and grazing programme, while lizard orchid and marsh helleborine are also to be found.

Summer provides an odd mixture on one part of the beach, however, where two colonies compete with each other for space: birds and nudists.

JUST WILD ABOUT FOOTBALL

Football teams and their natural nicknames:

AFC Bournemouth – The Cherries
Barnet – The Bees
Blackpool – The Tangerines
Bradford City – The Bantams
Brentford – The Bees
Brighton – The Seagulls
Bristol City – The Robins
Cardiff City – The Bluebirds
Cheltenham Town – The Robins
Chester City – The Seals
Derby County – The Rams
Huddersfield Town – The Terriers
Hull City – The Tigers
Leicester City – The Foxes
Mansfield Town – The Stags
Millwall – The Lions
Newcastle United – The Magpies
Norwich City – The Canaries
Notts County – The Magpies
Sheffield Wednesday – The Owls
Shrewsbury Town – The Shrews
Swansea City – The Swans
Swindon Town – The Robins
Torquay United – The Gulls
Watford – The Hornets
Wolverhampton Wanderers – The Wolves
Wrexham – The Robins

HOW ANCIENT IS ANCIENT?

We often talk about ancient woodland, but how old does an area have to be to qualify for such a title? The Woodland Trust provides the definition:

'Ancient woods are those where there is believed to have been continuous woodland cover since at least 1600 AD. Before this planting was uncommon, so a wood present in 1600 AD was likely to have developed naturally. In Scotland, ancient woodland sites are strictly those shown as semi-natural woodland on the 'Roy' maps, (a 1750 military survey and the best source of historical map evidence), and as woodland on all subsequent maps, however they have been combined with long-established woods of semi-natural origin (originating from between 1750 and 1860) into a single category of ancient woodland to take account of uncertainties in compilation of the ancient woodland inventory.

'Ancient semi-natural woodland (ASNW) is composed of native tree species that have not obviously been planted. Planted ancient woodland sites (PAWS) are ancient woods in which the former tree cover has been replaced, often with non-native trees. Important features of ancient woodland often survive in many of these woods, including characteristic flora and fauna, and archaeology.

'Our remaining ancient woodland covers less than 2% of the UK, and is irreplaceable.'

WINTER BLUES

Why is it we only see some species of butterfly, such as small tortoiseshell, during the winter, and not the rest? Butterflies have four life stages – egg, caterpillar, chrysalis and adult – and each species survives the winter months as one of these stages only (although one exception is the speckled wood, which gets through the cold months as either caterpillar or chrysalis).

Those that over-winter as eggs have thicker shells to withstand the cold, and in some cases release a fully formed caterpillar in the spring. Caterpillar species hibernate in vegetation, often by spinning a sleeping bag of thread among the leaves or blades in which to snuggle down, while those that use their chrysalis form tend to be found in thicker vegetation such as leaf litter. Finally, those that hibernate as adults may well take advantage of people's homes, sheds and lofts. Where none are available, thick patches of holly or ivy are the natural alternative.

Difference in size, in millimetres, between the great spotted and lesser spotted woodpeckers

YOU'RE SURE OF A BIG SURPRISE

Next time you're in south-east England, take a second look at that bird that's squawking at you from the trees above. The chances are greater than ever before that it's a member of the parrot family, in particular the ring-necked parakeet, that has been slowly developing feral colonies in Greater London, Kent and Sussex, but which has blossomed to a possible population of 4,500 thanks to the hot summer of 2003.

There's no doubt that Britain's warmer climes have encouraged the breeding success of this bird (can anyone still be in serious doubt about global warming?), but where did it come from in the first place? The most accepted belief is that a few broke out from private collections some 20-30 years ago, although more fascinating theories include the idea that some might have hitched a ride on the undercarriage of a London-bound jet (hence their prevalence in Richmond Park), or that today's entire population may have resulted from a pair that escaped during the filming of *The African Queen* at Shepperton Studios, starring Humphrey Bogart, Katherine Hepburn, and some parakeets.

GO DOWN IN NATURAL HISTORY

Wildlife named after great thinkers

Buddhaites – a mollusc
Confuciusornis sanctus – a dinosaur
Dalailama – a moth. It comes from Tibet
Lutheria and *Marxella* – wasp
Plato – a spider

NATURE NOTES

In a well-worn metaphor, a parallel is drawn between the life of man and the metamorphosis of the caterpillar into the butterfly; but the comparison may be more just as well as more novel, if for its former term we take the mental progress of the race. History shows that the human mind, fed by constant accessions of knowledge, periodically grows too large for its theoretical coverings, and bursts them asunder to appear in new habiliments, as the feeding and growing grub, at intervals, casts its too narrow skin and assumes another, itself but temporary. Truly the imago state of Man seems to be terribly distant, but every moult is a step gained, and of such there have been many.

Thomas H Huxley, *Man's Place in Nature*

HALF-TIME

The detail that goes into butterfly and moth illustration is extraordinary, and illustrators spend much of their lives peering into microscopes to study colour differentiations, scales and body structure. Yet since the advent of the printing process, help is at hand. Undamaged butterflies and moths are symmetrical, so illustrators only have to complete one side, and let the publishers do the rest. A very handy short cut with over 2,500 species in Britain alone to paint.

STRANGELY OMITTED FROM THE I-SPY BOOK OF ANIMALS

Manticore
Head of man, body of lion. Observe from side-on – if you stand in front, it will eat you, if you stand behind it will shoot spikes from its tail at you. Otherwise harmless. Score: 30 pts.

MEANWHILE, IN A FOREIGN LAND...

In the early years of 20th century Argentina, the belief that a family's seventh consecutive son could transform himself into a werewolf was so widely held that such offspring were being abandoned and even killed. To slow down the death rate, a law was passed in the 1920s stating that the president became automatic godfather of seventh sons, thus giving them their protection. The child would receive a gold medal on his day of baptism, and his schooling would be paid for until the age of 21.

The law is still in existence today, and presidents still occasionally attend the baptisms of seventh sons. Particularly in election year.

CRYPTIC CREATURES AND PUZZLING PLANTS

Unravel the following:
H
FLY
Answer on page 153

SITES FOR SORE EYES

Britain's wildlife isn't just land-based – some of the most fascinating sights the country has to offer are under water, and Purbeck Marine Wildlife Centre, off Dorset's Wareham coast, is a snorkeller's and rock-pooler's delight.

Unusually, the reserve, run by the Dorset Wildlife Trust, has a double low tide, offering plenty of opportunity for wildlife watching. Blenny, goby, pipe-fish, squat lobster and brittlestar are among the highlights of rockpool searches, while divers can enjoy watching cork-wing wrasse build their nests in the spring, or the beautiful pink sea fan at its most easterly known stronghold.

Yet if you're not too wild about submerging yourself in the water, no matter. The newly-built marine centre provides you with, among many other things, superb video links to the sights and colours of the Dorset underwater coast.

NATURE NOTES

Oyster shell when thrown at end turns up – as kestrel soaring, it rises as the onward force increases, at the moment when the impetus is just sufficient to act on the air and not sufficient to overcome it. So with birds' wing which is of oyster shell shape, so with boomerang. It is then the upstroke, the rising of the oyster, which supports the bird. For some reason that peculiar hollow form when driven forwards received from the air the maximum of support and rises as it were of itself as the soaring kestrel. Birds consequently whose wings nearest approach that shape – or a strip of it – as swallow and swift fly with the greatest ease and speed. The downstroke is deceptive it has led me to seek a power to strike the air downwards and so rise. Instead of which it is the unnoticed upstroke which effects suspension. What I have then to accomplish is not a vane striking down with great force and extreme velocity, but a form of wing adapted to allow suspension from the upstroke, and a mode of applying force which will give a sufficiently quick recovery for a second upstroke.

Richard Jeffries, *from his notebook dated July 8 1884.*
Jeffries, the Wiltshire naturalist, was preoccupied with trying to understand the power of flight during this time

A selection of fables in which animals teach us the true meaning of life.

The Hares and the Frogs
The Hares were so persecuted by the other beasts, they did not know where to go. As soon as they saw a single animal approach them, off they used to run. One day they saw a troop of wild Horses stampeding about, and in quite a panic all the Hares scuttled off to a lake hard by, determined to drown themselves rather than live in such a continual state of fear. But just as they got near the bank of the lake, a troop of Frogs, frightened in their turn by the approach of the Hares scuttled off, and jumped into the water. 'Truly,' said one of the Hares, 'things are not so bad as they seem'.
There is always someone worse off than yourself.

The Monkey and the Camel
The Beasts of the forest gave a splendid entertainment at which the Monkey stood up and danced. Having vastly delighted the assembly, he sat down amidst universal applause. The Camel, envious of the praises bestowed on the Monkey and desiring to divert to himself the favour of the guests, proposed to stand up in his turn and dance for their amusement. He moved about in so utterly ridiculous a manner that the Beasts, in a fit of indignation, set upon him with clubs and drove him out of the assembly.
It is absurd to ape our betters.

The Bat and the Weasel
A Bat who fell upon the ground and was caught by a Weasel pleaded to be spared his life. The Weasel refused, saying that he was by nature the enemy of all birds. The Bat assured him that he was not a bird, but a mouse, and thus was set free. Shortly afterwards the Bat again fell to the ground and was caught by another Weasel, whom he likewise entreated not to eat him. The Weasel said that he had a special hostility to mice. The Bat assured him that he was not a mouse, but a bat, and thus a second time escaped.
It is wise to turn circumstances to good account.

The Crab and the Fox
A Crab, forsaking the seashore, chose a neighbouring green meadow as its feeding ground. A fox came across him, and being very hungry ate him up. Just as he was on the point of being eaten, the Crab said, 'I well deserve my fate, for what business had I on the land, when by my nature and habits I am only adapted for the sea?'
Contentment with our lot is an element of happiness.

ANIMAL CRACKERS

Eystein, an 11th century north Norwegian king, was not a popular ruler. He made it his business to go around the neighbouring regions conquering the people and claiming their land as his own. The people of Throndhjem, however, were sturdier than most, and when Eystein installed his own son as king of their district, they killed him. Furious, Eystein returned to Throndhjem and offered the people a choice: their new king would either be Eystein's own slave Thorer Faxe, or his dog. The people chose the dog.

Saur, for that was the dog's name, ruled for three years. He lived in a mansion, wore a chain of gold, and was carried around by courtiers, who probably figured they were better off under him than under Eystein. His life ended when he heroically tried to save a herd of cattle from a pack of wolves, and was torn to bits.

10 COLEOPTERISTS (BEETLE-SPECIALISTS) WHO REALLY SHOULD HAVE STUDIED SOMETHING ELSE

Sir TH Beare
WA Beevor
TDA Cockerell
G Crabbe
PC Drake
Sir W Flower
KJ Fox
EA Heath
CG Lamb
JH Leech

And two who were born to the job:
W Lennon and JWH Harrison

QUOTE UNQUOTE

Nature does not say that cats are more valuable than mice; nature makes no remark on the subject. She does not even say that the cat is enviable or the mouse pitiable. We think the cat superior because we have (or most of us have) a particular philosophy to the effect that life is better than death. But if the mouse were a German pessimist mouse, he might not think that the cat had beaten him at all. He might think he had beaten the cat by getting to the grave first.
GK CHESTERTON, author

Number of books in the Collins New Naturalist series 85
by the end of the 20th century

Once viewed as so common that conservationists didn't have to worry about it, the house sparrow has suffered a mighty decline in recent years. Learned juries are still out on why this may be, but several theories are being explored:

Intensive farming – modern agricultural practices have reduced the amount of food available to birds during the winter.

Mobile phone masts – the rise in popularity of the mobile phone has coincided with the fall of the house sparrow population, leading some to believe that electromagnetic waves might be interfering with the bird's ability to reproduce or navigate.

Unleaded petrol – fumes given off by the substance might be hampering the survival rate of some of the sparrows' favourite insect foods.

Pesticides – by killing off aphids, pesticides not only reduce the number of ladybirds that feed on them, but the foodstuff that young sparrows need in their early years.

New building techniques – better insulation in our eaves may be reducing the birds' nesting opportunities.

Cats – the growing cat population tends to be more successful in killing ground-feeding birds, of which the house sparrow is a species.

NATURAL MYTHS

Mayflies only live for a day

Not true. They can live for up to a year as a developing larva; it is only in their adult, or imago stage, that life can last for just a matter of hours. The larvae lives in well-oxygenated waters, feeding on microscopic plants and detritus. Among other insects, moulting generally takes place during this stage, yet not with the mayfly. After perhaps a year of this slothlike development, life suddenly moves into fast-forward. A sub-imago emerges from the larval skin that then moults to become the full-grown adult. Males swarm to entice females towards them, then once mating has taken place, the female often drops its eggs back into the water. This has to happen quickly, as the adult mayfly is not able to feed. The eggs settle in the water or rocks, and the lengthy process with its frantic climax starts all over again.

QUOTE UNQUOTE

There is nothing in which the birds differ more from man than the way in which they can build and yet leave a landscape as it was before.
ROBERT LYND, sociologist

USEFUL WORDS TO KNOW WHEN MAMMAL-WATCHING

Den ....stoat home
Form ....hare home (slight depression in the ground)
Fortress........complex mole mound (large eruption in the ground)
Hoglet ....young hedgehog
Holt...otter home
Jill ....female polecat
Kit...young stoat
Kitten ....young rabbit
Latrine ....badger lavatory
Royal ....red deer stag with 12-pointed antlers
Scats ....fox droppings
Spraint ....otter droppings

HOPPING MAD

When it comes to jumping, the common froghopper – a frequent garden resident that hides its young in a froth called 'cuckoo-spit' – has the others beaten hands down. Only 6mm long, the little insect is capable of propelling its 12mg body 70cm into the air, exerting a force 400 times greater than its own body weight. This compares well with the exploits of a flea, whose force is around 135 times its body weight, a grasshopper, which can manage eight times, and a human, who can get up to about three times.

In addition:
- the froghopper accelerates in a millisecond up to a take-off velocity of 4m/second
- its initial acceleration is 4,000m/second
- the G-force it generates is more than 400 gravities, 80 times greater than that experienced by astronauts
- you need a 2,000 frame per second camera to record the jump
- the hind legs are so specialised for jumping that they are of no use for walking: the insect simply drags them behind itself.

THE BATS OF BRITAIN

Lesser horseshoe
Greater horseshoe
Whiskered
Brandts
Natterer's
Daubenton's
Bechstein's
Common pipistrelle
Soprano pipistrelle
Nathusius's pipistrelle
Brown long-eared
Grey long-eared
Barbastelle
Serotine
Noctule
Leisler's

NATURE NOTES

In early April, especially this cold spring, the hedgerows look misleadingly lifeless, the skeletons of the trees and bushes still without leaves. But much is happening or has happened already. Rabbits scurry along the hedges, and pheasants do the same, their colours merging into the pattern of the twigs. Hares with their March madness rely on their long legs to make a quick getaway across plough and grassland. Most self-respecting animals use the hedgerows as a highway from one destination to another. Hedgehogs are awake, hedge-sparrows are busy, the hedge-brown butterfly will not be about until later but you may see a small tortoiseshell, a peacock and even a brimstone. A lot of wild plants have 'hedge' in their name and I am making a list of them for my grandson in the hope that he will find them all before the year is over. There is a Jack-run-along-the-hedge growing all up our lane, with starry white flowers and leaves that smell of garlic when you crush them. Gerard recommends using this for sauce with your fish. The sweet-smelling violets will be in flower by now and so will the hedge-violets, otherwise known as dog-violets, but these lack any scent. In Somerset, Herb Robert is known as Jack-by-the-hedge; I know it as Robin's eye, and its leaf has a strong, slightly unpleasant smell.

There are many other hedge-named plants; bindweed is called hedge-bells and ground ivy hedge-maides. There is never any chance of missing goose grass; it will cling to you as its name, cleavers, indicates, but I have only just discovered that some people call it hedge-hogs.

Rosemary Verey, *A Countrywoman's Notes*

HOW TO FIND DORMICE

Dormice are nocturnal and keep themselves to themselves, so are very hard to see. Yet if you put in some decent research during the day, you can increase your chances. Your local Wildlife Trust can tell you which sites to find dormice in your area, but to find specific locations can require some detective work.

First of all, look out for evidence of nests (between autumn and spring only, so as not to disturb). Dormice construct them from shredded honeysuckle bark woven into a ball, often surrounded with layers of leaves. The home is a scruffy, loosely woven structure some four inches in diameter, generally fairly close to the ground. Low bramble bushes or thick undergrowth beneath trees with fruit such as hazel and sweet chestnut are the best habitats.

Evidence of fine dining is your second clue. Nibbled nuts are worth investigating – a dormouse leaves its hazels with a smooth inside surface, and toothmarks on the outside. Once you've established where the dormice are living, it may be time to lend a hand. Contact your local Wildlife Trust to find out how to encourage them further by putting up nestboxes.

Of course, you may be lucky and find one in your teapot.

AN OLD ELEPHANT JOKE?

Question: How do you cure an elephant of insomnia?

Answer: Rub into its shoulders a concoction of salt, olive oil and water.

If you're not laughing, that's because this isn't a joke, but a treatment prescribed by Aristotle himself for mahouts everywhere. The health of elephants seemed to have been quite a preoccupation of the thinkers of the ancient world. Solinus, for example, noted that should an elephant eat a chameleon by mistake, then it should chew quickly on an olive as an antidote to its poison – he recommended that people should do the same. Aristotle warned against excessive olive-consumption for elephants, however, particularly if they have been topping up on their iron content.

Meanwhile – Aristotle again – if you want your elephant to bear you boldly into war, the best way to stir up its passions is to give it grape or rice wine to get it fighting drunk.

The armadillo is one of the world's most fascinating creatures. It's been around for at least 55 million years, and its several species, of which the nine-banded is the most common, live in the southern states of the US and Latin America. How best to describe this curious armour-plated insect eater, that can consume up to 14,000 ants in one meal? The Aztecs called it Ayotochti, meaning rabbit-turtle; the naturalist John James Audubon in the mid-19th century described it as 'a small pig in the shell of a turtle'; its modern name derives from the Spanish for 'little armoured one'.

It has two ways of crossing a river. Although its armour plating weighs it down, it can gulp enough air to inflate its stomach and give it buoyancy. Alternatively, it is capable of holding its breath for up to six minutes, and just walk along the bottom.

Normal gestation takes around eight or nine months, yet if circumstances demand it, such as a change in climate, than the mother can delay giving birth for a further 20 months.

Because of its low body temperature, the armadillo is susceptible to the leprosy bacillus, which in humans concentrates in colder extremities such as fingers and toes, but nestles comfortably in the armadillos comparatively lukewarm parts.

QUOTE UNQUOTE

The fox has many tricks. The hedgehog has but one.
But that is the best of all.
DESIDERIUS ERASMUS, Dutch theologian

A NEW FLAVOUR IN HOSPITAL FOOD?

Garlic has long been known to keep Dracula at bay. Now, the miracle-worker has turned its attention to another creature that steals lives at night and is invisible by day. 'Hospital superbugs', as they've been dubbed, have become the scourges of today's medicine, mainly by infecting surgical wounds. MRSA (methicillin-resistant *Staphylococcus aureus*) kills up to 2,000 patients per year in Britain alone, and antibiotics have so far proved of little value in combating its strength.

Enter the garlic plant. Used in medicine for centuries, (as well as vampire-hunting), the herb contains Allicin, which has been discovered to be capable of killing MRSA and many others of the 'superbugs'. Another case of traditional medicines being the best?

STARLINGS MAKE A GREAT IMPRESSION

Starlings are one of the bird species that mimic other bird calls to show off their prowess to potential mates. Yet some birds have broader repertoires than others, mimicking:

Greenfinches
Magpies
Swallows
Cats
People's whistles
Mobile phones – Nokia is a particular favourite
Ice cream vans

PHENOLOGICALLY SPEAKING

The science of phenology is not new, but in recent years, it has begun to grow in importance. It's the study of the effect of changing patterns on naturally regular events, and in particular today, the effect of climate change on seasonal breeding and growth. Spring is one of the key times that phenological change is happening: the mean temperature from January to March in the 1960s was 4.2°C, whereas it stood at 5.6°C in the 1990s. This can have a disturbing effect on wildlife.

- Trees are leafing earlier than usual: horse chestnut shows the greatest advance of 12 days, oak 10 days and ash six.
- Butterflies are appearing earlier: the ringlet in particular is emerging one week earlier for every 1°C that average temperatures rise.
- Birds are migrating earlier: in 2002 swallows were arriving en masse over two weeks earlier than usual.
- More birds are coming here: several northern European species that usually fly to the Mediterranean in winter are now spending the colder months in a warmer Britain.

If you would like to put together your own lists of phenological observations, then visit the UK Phenology Network at www.phenology.org.uk.

BYRD SONG

The 11 members of the Byrds to make appearances on official albums:
Skip Battin • Gene Clark
Michael Clarke • David Crosby
Chris Hillman • Kevin Kelley
Roger McGuinn • Gene Parsons
Gram Parsons • Clarence White • John York

PLANTS WITH A BIT OF BOUNCE IN THEIR NAME

Spring crocus
Spring gentian
Spring snowflake
Spring squill
Spring vetch
Springbeauty

SITES FOR SORE EYES

It may not have the most prepossessing name, but the ECOS Millennium Environmental Centre is the centrepiece of one of Northern Ireland's finest nature reserves. Situated in Ballymena, Co Antrim, and run by the Ulster Wildlife Trust with Ballymena Borough Council, the reserve is grazed by rare Irish breeds of sheep and cattle, keeping the organically run meadows and grasslands perfect for breeding waders, skylarks and other ground-nesting birds. Sedge and grasshopper warblers breed on the reserve, while little grebe, teal and goldeneye are among the attractions of the lake during winter. The grasslands cover a wild spectrum of neutral and acid swards from dry, through peaty, to various states of dampness and periodic inundation.

The environmental centre itself provides information on how best to manage sites for the benefit of wildlife, as well as hints and ideas for sustainable living. You can even hire electrically charged bikes to get around.

NATURE NOTES

It was New Year's Eve. The old year was gone at last, according to the arbitrary measure we use to mark the passing of the years. I must go, my visit but an instant, an event of no significance whatever in the life of the field. Already its preparations for the New Year were well advanced. Some of the stinging nettles had fresh new leaves, some of the flowers were new, rather than fading blooms the autumn and winter winds had overlooked and on New Year's Eve itself, towards the top of the north-western, most antique hedge, where the gorse bushes were covered in pale grey buds, the first bright yellow flower had opened. Soon all the gorse would be covered with patches of yellow and, one by one, the other plants would begin to grow again. Slowly, regretfully, and yet not too slowly, for I was growing colder by the minute, I dropped the chain over the gate post, looked back once, crossed the road, and left.

Michael Allaby, *A Year in the Life of a Field*

Next time you're wandering around Middle Earth, see which of the following you can identify. Keep your distance.

Balrogs are evil spirits of fire that were among the first allies of Morgoth in the early days of Arda. Most were destroyed in the wars with elves and men, but a few remain, hidden away in the dark holes of the earth.

Crebain are large black crows that have been corrupted by evil.

Dumbledors are a species of giant wasp with bright black and yellow markings. Easily irritated, these animals have been known to swarm without provocation.

The giant eagles of Middle Earth are the greatest of all birds, nearly 12ft tall with a 35ft wingspan.

Ents (or the Onodrim) are huge plantlike humanoids who appear to be trees at a cursory glance. Although the oldest of the speaking races, it was the elves that taught the ents how to become mobile. They now act as caretakers of the forests and wild places.

Fell beasts resemble two-legged dragons with heads much like a vulture and two huge bat-like wings. The average specimen reaches about 30ft in length, with often a 40-50ft wingspan.

The Flies of Mordor are one of the few forms of life that actually thrives in Mordor. They are hideous creatures, almost an inch long, with the red mark of the Eye of Sauron on their backs.

Hummerhorns are huge mosquitoes, with a wingspan of nearly 4ft, and weighing almost 10lbs. Usually found in swamps and boggy areas, hummerhorns are fearless, and have been known to attack armoured knights.

Huorns are tree-like beings who live in forests tended by ents. They may look exactly like trees native to their particular forest, but are in fact either trees awakened from their sleep by ents, or ents who have slipped into dormancy.

Mearas are noble horses that live in the wilds of Middle Earth, occasionally serving as steeds for great lords. When urged to ride hard, they can cover nearly 25 miles an hour for up to 12 hours.

Mewlips are cannibalistic spirits that haunt mortals, feeding on their flesh and blood. They have horribly hunched backs, slanted eyes, sharp claws and teeth, and glistening brownish-gray skin.

Mumakil (sometimes called Oliphaunts) are huge, elephant-like beasts trained by the Haradrim as war beasts.

The great spiders of Middle Earth are truly monstrous creatures, possessing a high degree of sentience, and skilled in deception, stealth, and magic.

Trolls were bred by Morgoth in mockery of the ents. Huge, fearsomely strong, and belligerently stupid, trolls are a curse upon any that come across them.

Wargs are huge wolves infused with the power of first Morgoth, and later the Dark Lord. They have black fur, are much more intelligent than normal wolves, and some are even capable of speech.

SHOPPING THESE DAYS, IT'S A ZOO

Just click on the following to add to your trolley:
Famous Grouse whisky
Woodpecker cider
Penguin biscuits
Bird's Eye fish fingers
Animal biscuits
Doves Farm cereal bars
Fox's glacier mints
Dragonfly tea sachets
Tiger beer
Lyon's tea

ANIMAL CRACKERS

According to Sheila Ryan of Ohio, she has a gift: she can talk with animals, and horses in particular. Using a combination of metal dowsing rods and an understanding of spiritual points on the animal's body, she claims to be able to communicate in quite some detail. For example, Ryan was called in to help one rider find out why her horse was misbehaving at a show. After a little chat, she was able to report back that the horse was offended because its owner had been criticising it. The horse clearly felt that it shouldn't be jumping any more, too, because it apparently added: 'I'm older than you think I am'.

The psychologist (that's Ryan, not the horse), makes a pretty good living out of her holistic horse healing business, but she's quite the all-round linguist. In addition to English and Horse, she's fluent in Dog and Cat, too. She even once had a cosy little chat with a mountain lion.

GONE DOWN IN NATURAL HISTORY

Wildlife named after artists and writers

Microchilo elgrecoi – a moth.
Pseudoparamys cezannei – an extinct rodent.
Arthurdactylus conandoylensis – a pterosaur. So named because his story *The Lost World* is set in jungle similar to where the fossil was found.
Draculoides bramstokeri – a spider.
Legionella shakespearei – a bacterium.
Psephophorus terrypratchetti – a fossil turtle. Pratchett's fantasy world is carried on the back of such a beast.

SINGING FOR THEIR LIVES

Canaries were once commonly used as guinea-pigs to test whether subterranean mine-shafts had breathable air. Today, more technological means are used – where the mines are still in use – but occasionally the canaries still come into their own as saviours of mankind.

The December 2003 earthquake in Bam, Iran, cost the town at least 20,000 lives. The tally was two shorter than it might have been had not rescue workers been drawn to the chirping of two canaries trapped in the rubble. Moving the debris aside, they found two young children alongside the broken birdcage with the still singing canaries. Badly injured, the children were taken to hospital. The canaries were set free.

YOU'VE GOT SOME NECK!

It was once believed that if you walked slowly round and round a tree with an owl in it, the bird would watch you until it had wrung its own neck. Although owl necks can't turn quite that far, they do have the ability in some species to turn virtually 270° in either direction, thus being able to follow you three-quarters of the way round the tree. They can do this because they've got 14 neck vertebrae, twice as many as most mammals (including humans, giraffes, whales and mice).

But owl necks pale into significance alongside those of swans, however, which have up to 25 vertebrae. Even the mighty long-necked sauropods of millions of years ago, such as the 22m Mamenchisaurus, only had a maximum of 19.

NATURE NOTES

In that green country with its cool deep valleys and fantastic rocks, the narrow paths wind over the hills, linking village to hamlet; they cross streams and wander through woods with ancient names, a thousand intersecting paths, which have been used by the countryman from Saxon times. From the highest parts one can trace the grass-covered roads, along which no cart travels. There are curling hedges which hold protecting arms round odd little fields, and dark lichened stone walls cutting and dividing the green, and everywhere there are woods, beech woods, a flaming fire in the back end of the year, soft as clouds in spring, oak woods, rough and sturdy, plantations of dark fir and tender larch, and mixed woods of many colours and sounds, sheltering fox and badger, woods full of enchantment.

Alison Uttley, *Country World*

The Mother Shipton is a moth with patterning that resembles an old witch's face, giving the moth its name. Mother Shipton was a Yorkshire prophetess, born Ursula Sontheil in 1488 in a riverside cave at Knaresborough during a summer storm, and just a few feet away from the mysterious Petrifying Well which could turn objects to stone. Among the events she is alleged to have predicted are the Great Fire of London in 1666, the defeat of the Spanish Armada in 1588, and the advent of modern technology. She even forecast her own death in 1561.

Some, however, find her prophecies rather vague.
Judge for yourself:

Carriages without horses shall go.
And accidents fill the world with woe.
Around the world thoughts shall fly
In the twinkling of an eye...
Under water men shall walk,
Shall ride, shall sleep, shall talk;
In the air men shall be seen
In white, in black, and in green.
Iron in the water shall float
As easy as a wooden boat.

QUOTE UNQUOTE

I do not know what I may appear to the world; but to myself I seem to have been only like a boy playing on the seashore, and diverting myself in now and then finding a smoother pebble or a prettier shell than ordinary, whilst the great ocean of truth lay all undiscovered before me.
ISAAC NEWTON, scientist

ARABIAN WRITES

One of the earliest scientific natural history writers of the Arab world was Abu 'Uthman 'Amr ibn Bahr al-Kinani al-Fuqaimi al-Basri al-Jahiz – known simply as al-Jahiz – who was born in Basra in 776. As a youth, he worked with his father in the fish market, but his mother felt there was more to him. She gave him a collection of notebooks and suggested he try a career in writing.

He did. Launching with a study on the 'Institution of the Caliphate', he was taken in by the court of Baghdad, where he later moved. He wrote more than 200 works, including *The Art of Keeping One's Mouth Shut, Against Civil Servants, Arab Food*, and *In Praise of Merchants*, but it is for his *Book of Animals (Kitab al-Hayawan)* that he is best known today, an encyclopedia of seven large volumes.

The book contains an amazing array of scientific information. Al-Jahiz discusses his observation in detail on the social organisation of ants, and animal communication and psychology. He suggested an ingenious way of expelling mosquitoes and flies from a room based on his observation that some insects are responsive to light. He also observed that certain parasites adapt to the colour of their host, and expounded on the effects of diet and climate not only on men but also on animals and plants.

Al-Jahiz returned to Basra after spending more than 50 years in Baghdad. He died in Basra in 868 when a pile of books collapsed on him in his private library.

NATURAL MYTHS

Lemmings control their population by jumping off cliffs
Not true. Lemming population is, indeed, a very up-and-down affair, following a four-year cycle in which numbers increase by hundreds of percent, encouraging predator success, then crash as the predators become more successful. The cliff myth is based originally on the fact that Norwegian lemmings undertake great migrations about once every 30 years, in which they surge across the landscape in their thousands, jumping into rivers and sometimes falling off rocks to their doom through over-crowding, just as wildebeest do in their own annual migration. The myth was given apparent substance by Walt Disney in a 'factual' nature film called *White Wilderness* which showed lemmings leaping off apparent cliff edges. They were in fact being herded into a river from a man-made surface.

It is just like man's vanity and impertinence to call an animal dumb because it is dumb to his dull perceptions.
MARK TWAIN, US writer

RUDDY BAD LUCK

The ruddy duck, accidentally introduced into this country when a few pairs escaped from a wildfowl sanctuary in the 1950s, has settled down and made Britain its own in recent decades. This dapper little American, however, has caused an uproar in wildlife circles: it seems that some individuals are making their way to Spain and having their wicked way with a close cousin, the white-headed duck, a rare bird that cannot afford to have its bloodline diluted.

So what to do? The current plan is to kill them all, every last ruddy duck in Britain, for the sake of the white-headed duck. It's a plan that has conservationists and animal rights defenders split down the middle and at each other's throats.

Yet few – the ruddy ducks themselves apart, of course – are suffering more with the potential of this cull than the West Midlands Bird Club, whose symbol for some years has been no less than the ruddy duck. To bear a species on your logo that may shortly not exist in this country is an ill omen indeed, so recently, the club changed its logo to the one pictured. As you can see, the duck has gone.

Or has it...?

CRYPTIC CREATURES AND PUZZLING PLANTS

Which of the following is not a coastal fish:
Piddock, Pollack,
Lumpsucker, Father Lasher,
Gurnard?
Answer on page 153

COULD DRIVE YOU KWAKERS

Ducks go quack quack, right? Well, not necessarily.
Different languages describe the familiar call in different ways:

Albanian: mak mak	Hungarian: háp-háp
Bengali: gack-gack	Italian: qua qua
Croatian: kva-kva	Polish: kwa kwa
Danish: rap	Russian: krya-krya
Dutch: kwak kwak	Slovene: ga-ga
Estonian: prääks prääks	Spanish (Spain): cuá cuá
Finnish: kvaak kvaak	Turkish: vak, vak
French: coin coin	Ukrainian: krya-krya

ALBADROSS

Marine debris can be lethal to seabirds. Contents found in albatross
stomachs include:

Fishing net floats
A nine-inch piece of black plastic tubing
Fishing lures
Cigarette lighters
Toothbrushes
Sun lotion bottles
Inhalers
Soy sauce bottles
Toy planes and cars
A plastic dinosaur

NATURE NOTES

The air was wine, the moist earth-smell wine, the lark's song, the wafts
form the cowshed at the top of the field, the pant and smoke of a distant train – all were wine – or song, was it? or odour, this unity they all
blent into? I had no words then to describe it, that earth-effluence of
which I was so conscious; nor, indeed have I found words since. I ran
sideways, shouting; I dug glad heels into the squelching soil; I splashed
diamond showers from puddles with a stick; I hurled clods skywards at
random, and presently I somehow found myself singing. The words
were mere nonsense – irresponsible babble; the tune was an improvisa-
tion, a weary, unrhythmic thing of rise and fall: and yet it seemed to me
a genuine utterance, and just at that moment the one thing fitting and
right and perfect. Humanity would have rejected it with scorn. Nature,
everywhere singing in the same key, recognised and accepted it without
a flicker of dissent.

Kenneth Grahame, *The Golden Age*

Percentage of the British rabbit population killed by myxomatosis 99
in the 1950s

LEARNING FROM NATURE

Cockleburs produce small seed-bearing fruit covered with stiff, hooked spines. The spines have a purpose: by attaching themselves to fur or clothing, they are carried far and wide, distributing the plant around the world.

In 1948 amateur Swiss naturalist George de Mestral returned from a walk covered in burrs and, in a fit of curiosity, examined them. Looking at the burrs under a microscope, he noticed each one consisted of hundreds of tiny hooks that 'grabbed' onto loops of thread or fur. Inspired by their design, and realising that this hook and loop method could work equally well with clothing, he invented Velcro, short for 'velour crochet', or 'crocheted velvet'.

MEANWHILE, IN A FOREIGN LAND...

Africa's Grevy's zebra has suffered a disturbing decline in recent years, its Kenyan population alone falling by 70% in the 1980s. Unfortunately, rebuilding its numbers is a very slow process – the Grevy's has an extraordinarily slow gestation period of about 400 days.

Contrary to the belief that zebras are untameable, the Grevy's was the 'hippotigris' that pulled carts around arenas in Roman circuses in the 3rd century AD.

Each zebra has its own stripe pattern, rather like a human's fingerprints.

The creature is named after French president Jules Grevy (1813-1891) who was given three zebras as a gift by the King of Abyssinia, now Ethiopia.

SITES FOR SORE EYES

The mighty Chobham Common, run by the Surrey Wildlife Trust, is a true delight for lovers of heathland wildlife. Covered with sweeps of purple heather, amongst which are an array of mini-habitats, there's plenty to see. No fewer than 26 species of mammal live here – including the water vole – as do grass snakes, common and sand lizards. The site is also of UK importance for spiders, ladybirds, bees and wasps: keep an eye open, too, for Dartford warbler and hobby.

The reserve is rich in history. Its patchwork of habitats was first created by prehistoric farmers 6,000 years ago, while the common was given to the Abbot of Chertsey by sub-King Frithuwold in 676 AD. Queen Victoria herself reviewed her troops here before the Crimean War.

EIGHT-LEGGED CHAMELEONS

Britain has two species of octopus: the common, which can grow up to a metre in length, and the curled, which can manage about half that size. The common octopus is actually the least common of the two, but can be found in rocky coasts and lower shores in south-west Britain and the western region of the English Channel. A chameleon of the sea, it can change its colour from grey to brown to yellow to green depending upon its situation. The curled, or lesser octopus can be found in similar habitats, but along the entire British coastline. Its standard colour is a rusty brown, but it can also change rapidly depending upon its background.

PUTTING NAMES TO BIRDS' BITS

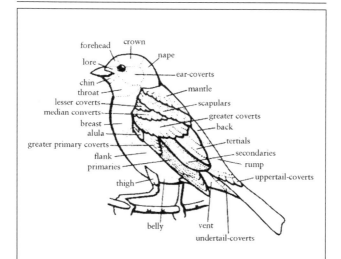

Sometimes, when you only get a brief glimpse of a bird, there's no chance to look at the detail above. At these times, taking habitat, season and call (if heard) into account, experienced birdwatchers use 'jizz'. This is the 'character' of the bird, nothing you can put your finger on exactly, but enough to recognise a familiar species, just as you can recognise a friend's voice. The word probably comes from the air pilots' phrase to identify other aircraft: General Impression, Size and Shape, shortened to GISS, and pronounced 'jizz'.

CUTE LITTLE CRACKERS

Do you remember those little porcelain animals that used to fall out of Christmas crackers or nestle at the bottom of teabag boxes? Wade Whimsies, for so they are called, were one of the most enduring collectables of the second half of the 20th century, celebrating their 50th anniversary in 2003.

The figures – pets, British countryside animals, African wildlife and so on – were first produced by Wade Ceramics of Burslem, Stoke-on-Trent in the 1950s as miniature versions of pre-war designs, aimed at the children's market. They were so successful that 50 were produced in the 1950s, and a further 60 in the 1970s.

And they're still in production, with new designs appearing regularly. Today, collectors fall over themselves at international get-togethers to pick up the rarities, which can fetch dozens of pounds in good condition.

IT'S IN THE BLOOD

Moles are mammals, yet they can pursue hugely active lives tunnelling away under the earth where oxygen is not so much thin on the ground, as thin in it. How do they do this? The answer lies in the blood. They have twice as much of it, and twice as much haemoglobin, as other mammals their size. In addition, the haemoglobin has a further enhanced ability when it comes to soaking up whatever oxygen it can find, turning the little creature into a virtual velvet sponge.

But moles aren't alone in this adaptation. On the other side of the world, in the high Andean mountains where oxygen is thin in the air, llamas have developed a similarly efficient internal blood system to cope with their environment.

CAUGHT A CRAB?

In 1993, Greenland issued a new series of stamps to celebrate its wildlife, one of which was the Saatuaq crab. There, on the 7.25-krone stamp was a fine picture of the crustacean, complete with its scientific name *Chionoecetes oiliqo*.

Complaints came in: the Latin was wrong, badly wrong. The name should have been *C. opilio*. The printers went back to their plates, and spotted their mistake. They had accidentally reversed the specific name, ending up with a mirror image: opilio – oiliqo.

GONE DOWN IN NATURAL HISTORY

Wildlife named after famous people

Mastagophora dizzydeani – a spider.
Named after a baseball player. The spider uses a sticky ball to
catch its prey.

Campsicnemius charliechaplini – a fly. Named for the tendency of
the fly to die in a bandy-legged position.

Baeturia laureli and B. hardyi – cicadas.

Bufonaria borisbeckeri – a sea snail.

Strigiphilus garylarsoni – a louse. The cartoonist wrote later:
'You have to grab these opportunities when they come along. I
knew no-one was going to name a new species of swan after me.'

Sula abbotti costelloi – a subspecies of Abbot's booby, (similar to a
gannet), although now extinct.

Sylvilagus palustris hefneri – a marsh rabbit. Only Hugh Hefner
could have a bunny named after him.

Godiva – a nudibranch. Nudibranches are marine molluscs with
exposed, or naked, gills.

NATURE NOTES

Feel like a piece of drawn threadwork, or an undeveloped negative, or
a jellyfish on stilts, or a sloppy tadpole, or a weevil in a nut, or a spitch-
cocked eel. In other words and in short – ill.

…The doctor's orders 'cease work' have brought on in an aggravated
form my infatuation for zoological research. I lie in bed and manufac-
ture rolling periods in praise of it, I get dithyrambic over the zoologists
themselves — Huxley, Wallace, Brooks, Lankester. I chortle to reflect
that in zoology there are no stock exchange ambitions, there is no mention of slum life, Tariff Reform is not included. In the repose of the spa-
cious laboratory by the seaside or in the halls of some great museum,
life with its vulgar struggles, its hustle and obscenity, scarcely penetrates. Behind those doors, life flows slowly, deeply. I am ascetic and
long for the monastic seclusion of a student's life.
WNP Barbellion, *The Journal of a Disappointed Man, 1911*

CATERWAULING

A list of feline chart-toppers:
Tiger Feet – Mud
The Cat Crept In – Mud again
The Lion Sleeps Tonight – Many, many artists
What's New Pussycat? – Tom Jones
Cool for Cats – Squeeze
Eye of the Tiger – Survivor
Three Lions (Football's Coming Home) – Lightning Seeds
Everybody wants to be a Cat – Phil Harris and
Scatman Crothers (The Aristocats)
Feline Groovy – Simon and Garfunkel
Anything by Atomic Kitten, Cat Stevens, Eartha Kitt or Lionel Ritchie.

MALE PATTERN BEHAVIOUR

Although both genders bear the name, to talk of a female mallard is, to be pedantic about it, something of an oxymoron. The species itself was once known simply as the wild duck, only the drake being called the mallard, the word deriving from older forms of 'male'. This bird, the ancestor of many of today's domestic ducks, certainly lives a testosterone-filled life. Pairing in autumn, mallards are very protective of their mates, but will take any opportunity they can to continue their bloodline with another female. It is not unusual for several males to group around another drake's mate and force her to copulate with them. So aggressive is the event that females have been known to die as a result.

Meanwhile, once their own eggs have hatched, the drakes leave the females to look after the family. Comparisons with another species should only be tentatively drawn.

A TURNER FOR THE BOOKS

William Turner (1508-68) has been dubbed the Father of British Botany for his extensive cataloguing of British flora. He was the first to publish the names of several plants: among today's rarities to be first recorded by Turner are:
Corncockle
Dittander
Pasqueflower
Pheasant's eye
Thorow-wax
Wild cabbage
Wild pear

...there's a Wildlife Trust looking after dozens of reserves nearby. The contact details for the The Wildlife Trusts, and each of the 47 individual Trusts are as follows:

The Wildlife Trusts UK Office
Tel 0870 0367711
www.wildlifetrusts.org

Alderney Wildlife Trust
Tel 01481 822935
www.wildlife.alderney.com

Avon Wildlife Trust
Tel 0117 917 7270
www.avonwildlifetrust.org.uk

Berks, Bucks and Oxon Wildlife Trust
Tel 01865 775476
www.bbowt.org.uk

Brecknock Wildlife Trust
Tel 01874 625 708
www.wildlifetrust.org.uk/brecknock

Cheshire Wildlife Trust
Tel 01270 610 180
www.wildlifetrust.org.uk/cheshire

Cornwall Wildlife Trust
Tel 01872 273 939
www.cornwallwildlifetrust.org.uk

Cumbria Wildlife Trust
Tel 01539 816300
www.cumbriawildlifetrust.org.uk

Derbyshire Wildlife Trust
Tel 01773 881188
www.derbyshirewildlifetrust.org.uk

Devon Wildlife Trust
Tel 01392 279 244
www.devonwildlifetrust.org

Dorset Wildlife Trust
Tel 01305 264620
www.wildlifetrust.org.uk/dorset

Durham Wildlife Trust
Tel 0191 584 3112
www.wildlifetrust.org.uk/durham

Essex Wildlife Trust
Tel 01621 862960
www.essexwt.org.uk

Gloucestershire Wildlife Trust
Tel 01452 383333
www.gloucestershirewildlifetrust.co.uk

Gwent Wildlife Trust
Tel 01600 715501
www.wildlifetrust.org.uk/gwent

Hampshire and Isle of Wight
Tel 02380 613636
www.hwt.org.uk

Herefordshire Nature Trust
Tel 01432 356872
www.wildlifetrust.org.uk/hereford

Hertfordshire and Middlesex
Tel 01727 858901
www.wildlifetrust.org.uk/herts

Isles of Scilly Wildlife Trust
Tel 01720 422153
www.ios-wildlifetrust.org.uk

Kent Wildlife Trust
Tel 01622 662012
www.kentwildlife.org.uk

Leicestershire and Rutland
Tel 0116 272 0444
www.lrwt.org.uk

Lincolnshire Wildlife Trust
Tel 01507 526667
www.lincstrust.org

London Wildlife Trust
Tel 0207 261 0447
www.wildlondon.org.uk

contd...

Manx Wildlife Trust
Tel 01624 801985
www.wildlifetrust.org.uk/
manxwt

Montgomeryshire Wildlife Trust
Tel 01938 555654
www.montwt.co.uk

Norfolk Wildlife Trust
Tel 01603 625540
www.wildlifetrust.org.uk/norfolk

North Wales Wildlife Trust
Tel 01248 351541
www.wildlifetrust.org.uk/
northwales

Northumberland Wildlife Trust
Tel 0191 2846884
www.wildlifetrust.org.uk/
northumberland

Nottinghamshire Wildlife Trust
Tel 0115 958 8242
www.wildlifetrust.org.uk/
nottinghamshire

Radnorshire Wildlife Trust
Tel 01597 823298
www.waleswildlife.co.uk

Scottish Wildlife Trust
Tel 0131 312 7765
www.swt.org.uk

Sheffield Wildlife Trust
Tel 0114 263 4335
www.wildlifetrust.org.uk/sheffield

Shropshire Wildlife Trust
Tel 01743 284280
www.shropshirewildlifetrust.
org.uk

Somerset Wildlife Trust
Tel 01823 451587
www.wildlifetrust.org.uk/somerset

Staffordshire Wildlife Trust
Tel 01889 880100
www.staffs-wildlife.org.uk

Suffolk Wildlife Trust
Tel 01473 890089
www.wildlifetrust.org.uk/suffolk

Surrey Wildlife Trust
Tel 01483 795440
www.surreywildlifetrust.co.uk

Sussex Wildlife Trust
Tel 01273 492630
www.sussexwt.org.uk

Tees Valley Wildlife Trust
Tel 01642 759900
www.wildlifetrust.org.uk/teesvalley

The Wildlife Trust for
Bedfordshire, Cambridgeshire,
Northamptonshire and
Peterborough
Tel 01223 712400
www.wildlifebcnp.org

The Wildlife Trust for Birmingham
and the Black Country
Tel 0121 454 1199
www.bbcwildlife.org.uk

The Wildlife Trust for
Lancashire, Manchester and
North Merseyside
Tel 01772 324129
www.wildlifetrust.org.uk/lancashire

The Wildlife Trust of South and
West Wales
Tel 01656 724100
Email glamorganwt@cix.co.uk

Ulster Wildlife Trust
Tel 02844 830282
www.ulsterwildlifetrust.org

Warwickshire Wildlife Trust
Tel 024 7630 2912
www.warwickshire-wildlife-trust-
org.uk

Wiltshire Wildlife Trust
Tel 01380 725670
www.wiltshirewildlife.org

Worcestershire Wildlife Trust
Tel 01905 754919
www.worcswildlifetrust.co.uk

Yorkshire Wildlife Trust
Tel 01904 659570
www.yorkshire-wildlife-trust.org.uk

SMELL A RAT?

One of the greatest mammalian success stories is that of the brown rat. By the year 1700, the animal was not found west of the Volga, but some believe that an Asian earthquake helped to get its population moving, and within a short time, it had made first Russia, then Europe its own, reaching:

- Denmark in 1716
- Britain in 1720 (probably on a Russian timber ship)
- Ireland in 1722
- France in 1750
- Norway in 1762 (although their Latin name is *Rattus norvegicus*, they did not reach this land until comparatively late)
- Spain and Italy in the early 19th century.

By 1777, the natural historian Gilbert White had noted that the black rat, which was being steadily replaced by the 'Norwegian' newcomer, was already becoming a 'newcomer'. Today it has a British population of some seven million.

IMAGINE THESE TUNNELLING UNDER YOUR FLOWERBEDS

The word 'mammoth' has entered the vernacular in such a way that its hard to believe that it could ever have meant anything other than 'pretty darn big'. Yet the root of the word probably comes from the Estonian meaning 'earth-mole'.

Mammoths, whose carcasses survived the Ice Age through preservation in permafrost, frequently turned up through the millennia since their extinction half-buried in the ground – indeed, Siberia still hosts some examples. As extinct creatures were unknown, people presumed that the mammoth still existed, and as no one ever saw a live one, they were believed to be subterranean creatures that, should they accidentally tunnel to the surface, would die upon contact with the air. In some parts of Siberia, the myth still exists today, and newly found remains are quickly destroyed as the 'earth-mole' is deemed to bring bad luck.

QUOTE UNQUOTE

If a man walks in the woods for love of them half of each day, he is in danger of being regarded as a loafer. But if he spends his days as a speculator, shearing off those woods and making the earth bald before her time, he is deemed an industrious and enterprising citizen.
HENRY DAVID THOREAU, naturalist and writer

NATURE NOTES

My own belief is that the natural world cannot be evaluated simply in terms of scientific criteria. Nor can it be dismissed as an arena for the amusement of naturalists. Even broader comparisons – for instance with our heritage of art treasures – can be misleading, and return us to that image of a static museum, a collection of living fossils, from which we have had to argue our way clear. The natural world is ubiquitous; it is too pervasive, too much alive to be contained within any of these models. It touches us all, physically and emotionally, in every aspect of our lives, even when we are not aware of it.

Richard Mabey, *The Common Ground*

MEANWHILE, IN A FOREIGN LAND...

The rarest parrot in the world is also the largest, and quite probably the strangest, too. New Zealand is famous for hosting the kiwi, but it's also home to the flightless kakapo, an 8lb parrot that once roamed the islands in its hundreds of thousands, but now is reduced to a few dozen individuals, thanks to its defencelessness against introduced predators, including man.

Before 1845, which was when Europeans first clapped eyes on the kakapo, (known also as the owl-parrot for its nocturnal habits and facial resemblance), Maoris used the bird for meat and its feathers for cloaks, yet the population still remained fairly stable. The gold-diggers of the late 19th century lived in some cases on a diet of nothing but kakapo – rather bravely, as the bird has a strong, musky scent.

This wonderful bird possesses a haunting booming call, uttered at a low frequency and backed by occasional screeching. It also breeds on average only once every two to four years.

TEASEL DO

Teasel is unique in the plant world in the way in which it blooms. Its flowers first appear in a ring around the middle of the head, and spread slowly outwards. As the blooms are fairly short-lived, the new growths outlive the central growths, effectively creating two further rings that move slowly towards the top and bottom of the head. By the time the plant has released all its seeds, it dies leaving behind a tough structure surrounded by stiff, sharp bristles. This makes it the ideal tool for 'teasing' wool, a process practised since Roman times.

NATURAL MYTHS

Bread and milk is good for hedgehogs

Not true. Hedgehogs will lap it up, but they shouldn't be eating it.
The bread can swell in the stomach, causing potential intestinal problems for the animal, while milk contains lactose of which many animals are intolerant, causing diarrhoea and possibly dehydration.

Milk can also harbour bacteria for which a hedgehog has no tolerance. During summer months, hedgehogs need to drink plenty of water, but if they assuage their thirst with milk, they could suffer from dehydration. (One observer in June 1997 watched a hedgehog lapping at water continually for 75 minutes, the animal averaging three laps per second.) Finally, of course, if left outside too long on a summer night, the milk might curdle.

No, bread and milk is not good for hedgehogs.

ANIMAL CRACKERS

It was late one Pennsylvania night in 2000 and the Beck family were fast asleep. They heard knocking at their front door, and wondered what was going on. Suddenly, the door was flung open, and something came running heavily up the stairs. Nervously, they tiptoed from the bedroom towards the bathroom where the thing could be heard crashing around frantically. Closing the door on it, they called the police, while inside the bathroom could be heard the sound of something kicking on a tap. As the bath filled with water, the crashing became a splashing – the sound of breaking bottles soon joined it. When the police arrived, they cautiously opened the door. A panicking deer was thrashing around in a bubble bath it had accidentally run for itself.

STAMPED OUT

In 1998, the Royal Mail issued a series of commemorative stamps to highlight the plight of some of Britain's endangered species. Found on the stamps were portraits of:

Common dormouse	20p
Lady's slipper orchid	26p
Song thrush	31p
Shining ram's-horn snail	37p
Mole cricket	41p
Devil's bolete	63p

Interestingly, Consignia was not on the list.

MAN DEFINED

How to get from every creature that's ever lived
to mankind in just eight easy steps:

Kingdom: *Animalia*
Phylum: *Chordata*
Subphylum: *Vertebrata*
Class: *Mammalia*
Order: *Primates*
Family: *Hominidae*
Genus: *Homo*
Species: *sapiens*
Subspecies: *sapiens sapiens*

WHERE HAVE ALL THE FLOWERS GONE?

In 2000, naturalist Peter Marren compiled a list of lost flora in
English counties during the previous, approximately, hundred years.

County	Species lost during recording period	Recording period
Northamptonshire	93	1930-1995
Gloucestershire	78	1900-1986
Lincolnshire	77	1900-1985
Middlesex	76	1900-1990
Durham	68	1900-1988
Essex	68	1862-1974
Cambridgeshire	66	1900-1990
Avon	65	1900-2000
Leicestershire	59	1900-1988
Surrey	51	1900-1986
Suffolk	50	1900-1982
Cheshire	49	1900-1990
Cumberland	48	1900-1997
Bedfordshire	42	1900-1980
Norfolk	33	1900-1999

CRYPTIC CREATURES AND PUZZLING PLANTS

Change the bold letter in each word to make a new word, while turning
a drink into a fruit when the five new letters are read downwards.

	J	UST
N	**U**	T
	L	IME
P	**E**	ACH
	P	EAR

Answer on page 153

NATURE NOTES

When he reached the place he was aiming for, he began making holes in the ground with his rod, putting an acorn in each and then covering it up again. He was planting oak trees. I asked him if the land was his. He said it wasn't. Did he know who the owner was? No, he didn't. He thought it must be common land, or perhaps it belonged to people who weren't interested in it. He wasn't interested in who they were. And so, with great care, he planted his hundred acorns.

After the midday meal he started sorting out more acorns to sow. I must have been very pressing with my questions, because he answered them. He'd been planting trees in this wilderness for three years. He'd planted a hundred thousand of them. Out of those, twenty thousand had come up. Of the twenty thousand he expected to lose half, because of rodents or the unpredictable ways of Providence. That still meant then thousand oaks would grow where before there had been nothing.

It was at this point that I wondered how old he was. He was obviously over fifty. Fifty-five, he said. His name was Elzeard Bouffier. He had once owned a farm on the plains. It was there he had lived his life.

But he had lost first his only son, then his wife. After that he came here to be alone, enjoying an unhurried existence with his sheep and his dog. But it struck him that this part of the country was dying for lack of trees, and having nothing much else to do he decided to put things right.

Jean Giono, *The Man who Planted Trees*

SITES FOR SORE EYES

After 1066, life wasn't as easy for William the Conqueror as he might have supposed. The south and east of England fell under his boot reasonably easily, but the northern region fought hard against Norman dominion. His response was forthright: he burnt and devastated the land between York and Durham in a ferocious period from 1069 to 1970 known as 'harrying the north', until the rebellion was subdued.

Coatham Marsh near Redcar was a site of one of the battles of that period, yet in the intervening centuries, nature has stepped back in to restore it as its own once more. Now managed by the Tees Valley Wildlife Trust, Coatham Marsh is a fine example of nature thriving on the urban fringe: its wetland features attract a broad diversity of birds, particularly during migration periods and winter, while dragonflies are a delight during the warmer months. Swathes of orchids adorn the grasslands during the summer. Meanwhile, some of the smaller mounds are remnants of another ancient man-made disturbance – medieval salt workings.

In 2001, a pair of choughs – coastal crows with long, curved, tomato-red beaks – were about to be released from captivity in an attempt to get the species breeding in Cornwall for the first time in nearly 50 years. A prime site had been picked. Due to Foot and Mouth Disease, however, the programme was delayed, and in the meantime, some wild choughs flew in, nested in a different site that had not been deemed worthy, and raised four chicks. Peter Marren, one of the UK's finest commentators on conservation issues, when investigating the story, was told that the wild choughs were responding to 'appropriate management'. It was as if, although the birds had drawn up their own breeding programme, mankind still had to demonstrate some overall control. 'Could it be', Marren pondered in *British Wildlife* magazine, 'that the satisfaction of bringing back a lost animal by dint of careful planning and preparation is greater than that of merely witnessing a natural event?'

BROCK STARS

How to find out if there's a badger sett in your vicinity. If you do find one, however… don't badger it.

- Badger setts tend to be D-shaped, larger than fox-holes, and with little if any food outside the entrance.
- Steam rising from the sett on cold winter days.
- Badger foot-prints can often be smudged, as the animal tends to put its hind paw on the same spot as the fore paw.
- Badgers are notoriously clean creatures, so look out for piles of old plant bedding, latrines and small bones. A sett is likely to be nearby.
- Scratch marks on nearby trees or posts.
- Reasonably obvious pathways, as badgers follow set routes every night.
- Round, shallow snuffle-holes, where the badgers have been searching for worms.
- Torn up wasp nests.
- Badger hair on barbed wire fences. The hair is black and white, about 10cm long, and rough to the touch.

QUOTE UNQUOTE

The Creator has an inordinate fondness for beetles.
JBS HALDANE, naturalist

IF YOU GO DOWN TO THE WOODS TODAY

Want to make a wooden object? Then you need the right type of
wood. Traditional uses for different woods include:

Alder	Clogs and broom handles. Fencing
Ash, Common	Oars, paddles, tool shafts and handles walking sticks, arrow shafts
Beech, Common	Mallets. Yokes
Black Poplar	Matchsticks
Blackthorn	Walking sticks, rake teeth. Chessmen
Damson	Cabinet making
Elder	Spoons
Oak	Furniture, house beams, ships
Hazel	Hurdles, basketry, crate hoops, building material
Hornbeam	Mallet heads, chopping blocks, yokes, wheel spokes
Laburnum	Cabinet making
Lime	Musical instruments, spoons
Rowan	Tool handles and carving
Scots Pine	Furniture, railway sleepers
Silver Birch	Broom bristles, tool handles
Sycamore	Furniture, musical instruments, household utensils
Walnut	Furniture
White Willow	Cricket bats, trugs
Wild Cherry	Tobacco pipes
Yew	Bows

THREE MEN AND A BOOK

Kenneth Grahame, a Scottish
secretary to the Bank of
England, was fond of telling
stories about a character called
Toad to his son, Alastair, who
was born in 1900. Alastair
was fond of hearing them, too;
so much so that Grahame
decided to get the tales
published and try them out on
a wider market. *The Wind in
the Willows* was published in
1908, although initially only
to a lukewarm reception. As
the years went by, its
popularity slowly grew,
however, and AA Milne and
EH Shepherd, writer and
illustrator of the tales of
Winnie the Pooh, became
interested. Shepherd illustrated
the book, and Milne
dramatised it for the stage as
Toad of Toad Hall.

Unlike Milne's own son
Christopher Robin, however,
Alastair Grahame was not to
live to see the great success
that his childhood tales
spawned. He was killed in the
Great War.

The animals and plants of Aesop's Fables help us learn to take the rough with the smooth.

The Rose and the Amaranth

A Rose and an Amaranth blossomed side by side in a garden, and the Amaranth said to her neighbour, 'How I envy you your beauty and your sweet scent! No wonder you are such a universal favourite.' But the Rose replied with a shade of sadness in her voice, 'Ah, my dear friend, I bloom but for a time: my petals soon wither and fall, and then I die. But your flowers never fade, even if they are cut; for they are everlasting.'

Greatness carries its own penalties.

The Raven and the Swan

A Raven saw a Swan and desired to secure for himself the same beautiful plumage. Supposing that the Swan's splendid white colour arose from his washing in the water in which he swam, the Raven left the altars in the neighbourhood where he picked up his living, and took up residence in the lakes and pools. But cleansing his feathers as often as he would, he could not change their colour, while through want of food he perished.

Change of habit cannot alter nature.

The Fox and the Bramble

A Fox was mounting a hedge when he lost his footing and caught hold of a Bramble to save himself. Having pricked and grievously torn the soles of his feet, he accused the Bramble because, when he had fled to her for assistance, she had used him worse than the hedge itself. The Bramble, interrupting him, said, 'But you really must have been out of your senses to fasten yourself on me, who am myself always accustomed to fasten upon others.'

To the selfish all are selfish

The Ant and the Grasshopper

In a field one summer's day a Grasshopper was hopping about, chirping and singing to its heart's content. An Ant passed by, bearing along with great toil an ear of corn he was taking to the nest. 'Why not come and chat with me,' said the Grasshopper, 'instead of toiling and moiling in that way?' 'I am helping to lay up food for the winter,' said the Ant, 'and recommend you to do the same.' 'Why bother about winter?' said the Grasshopper; 'we have got plenty of food at present.' But the Ant went on its way and continued its toil. When the winter came the Grasshopper had no food and found itself dying of hunger, while it saw the Ants distributing every day corn and grain from the stores they had collected in the summer.

It is best to prepare for the days of necessity.

CRYPTIC CREATURES AND PUZZLING PLANTS

Unravel the following:
BET
Y

Answer on page 153

BY NAME, BY NATURE

The swift, one of our shorter-staying summer visitors, is the most aerial of birds. It feeds, sleeps, drinks and even mates on the wing, alighting only to build its nest, incubate the eggs and feed its young. The mating occurs at a great height, for they need a long way to fall during the process. The female flies in front of the male in a horizontal flight, and he lands on top of her with his own wings held high. They move their tails back and forth in an attempt to mate, while dropping steadily. This is one of nature's only mating procedures that, should it last too long, could end in death.

This is compounded by the fact that swifts are incapable of slow flight. Their lengthy carpus bones account for their very long primary feathers. These are the feathers that produce a downward and forward thrusting force, helpful for speed, but not so useful for manoeuvrability and subtler flight. Yet manoeuvrability is not so necessary when you barely come lower than rooftop level. Most things at that height and above tend not to move suddenly – apart from other birds. Swifts have been recorded at surprisingly old ages for such small birds, up to 21 in fact, and one of the oldest found had been killed in a collision... with another swift.

RAGGING ON RAGWORT

Ragwort is becoming quite an issue in Britain. The plant, with its bright yellow petals, resembles a golden daisy (to which it is related), but its attractive appearance belies an unfortunate side-effect: it is toxic to livestock. Horses, ponies and donkeys in particular are susceptible to it, and can develop potentially fatal liver damage from eating it, even if only through seeds drifting into their hay. As a result, the British Horse Society and the government have been promoting a *Ragwort Control Bill* to prevent its spread.

Yet ragwort has its admirers, too. The caterpillar of the cinnabar moth feeds off the plant, and takes on the toxic properties itself, which it advertises to potential predators via its own warning system, a heavily marked black and yellow body. Many believe that the moth could suffer through excessive clearance of ragwort. The case is a classic example of conservation versus animal welfare.

A CROW BY ANY OTHER NAME

Country names for the hooded crow:
Cawdy mawdy
Denman
Dunbilly
Harry Dutchman
Isle of Wight crow
Kentishman
Market Jew crow
Royston Dick

LORDS OF THE FAIRY RINGS

Britain has at least 12,000 species of fungi, but unless you know your Latin, you'd be hard pressed to name very many of them. So, in 2000, the Fungus Conservation Forum bestowed English names to around 1,000 species of fungi. Mycology should be easier than ever... although some of species do now sound strangely like minor characters dreamt up by Tolkien:

Asterophora parasitica	Silky piggyback
Amanita virosa	Destroying angel
Boletus pseudoregius	The pretender
Chlorociboria aeruginascens	Green elfcup
Collybia peronata	Wood woollyfoot
Craterellus cornucopioides	Horn of plenty
Cudonia confusa	Cinnamon jellybaby
Hymenoscyphus fructigenus	Nut disco
Laetiporus sulphureus	Chicken of the woods
Melanotaenium endogenum	Bedstraw smut
Omphalina chlorocyanea	Verdigris navel
Porpoloma metapodium	Mealy meadowcap
Russula rosea	Rosy brittlegill
Russula vesca	The flirt
Stropharia coronilla	Garland roundhead
Tricholoma sejunctum	Deceiving knight
Xylaria carpophila	Beechmast candlesnuff

YOU DIDN'T NEED TO KNOW THESE, BUT...

The skin of a polar bear is black
Rats cannot vomit
Porcupines float in water
If an octopus becomes excessively stressed it might eat itself
Ants stretch when they wake up
Some lions will mate over 50 times a day

MEANWHILE, IN A FOREIGN LAND...

When news spread a few years ago that the tiny town of Talkeetna in Alaska hosts an annual moose dropping festival, animal activists began to sweat. This, surely, was worse even than bear-baiting and cock-fighting.

Not so. The festival celebrates not the chucking of moose off a cliff, but the animals' droppings themselves. They're thrown from a balloon, the closest to a target winning prizes. This event takes place during the second week of every July, after which the inch-long brown pellets are shellacked and sold in vast quantities to curious tourists who snap up the turds and take them home as novelty earrings, Christmas decorations, necklaces and swizzle sticks.
Cocktail, anyone?

NATURE NOTES

In the summer night such marauders as are about – the night insects, the rabbit nibbling clover on the lawn, the slug sucking the iris blade – all go about their work of destruction in a single-minded silence. Sleep is disturbed not by noises but by the moonlight on the bedroom floor. But in the late fall and early winter, especially before the snow comes, there is a time of terror when field mice, rats, and squirrels, driven indoors by the cold, make ratching-scratching sounds inside the walls; the stairs creak; some part of the house settles a thousandth of an inch (the effect of a dead man's curse or a witch in the neighbourhood); and people whose dreams are too active wake and hear sounds that (so the pounding in their left side tells them) have been made by a prowler.
William Maxwell, *Time will Darken it*

NAVIGATIONAL SYSTEMS FOR MICE

How do mice, as they scurry about at night, know whether or not they're exploring new areas, or simply scurrying round and round the same spot. According to some recent research, they could be using their own landmarks.

Researchers discovered that when wood mice came across an item that differed from most others in an environment, such as, in one experiment, a plastic white disc, it would drag it to the area where it was foraging, then scamper off. After a while, it would return to the disc, then run off in a different direction. It appeared to be using the disc as a landmark to focus its energies more efficiently. Yet plastic white discs are not all that common in the wild, so mice have to make their own landmarks. One common approach is to drag a number of leaves into a small yet distinct pile.

YOU'RE SURE OF A BIG SURPRISE

Grazing animals such as cattle and sheep are common agents of conservation in Britain... but water buffalo? These European imports have for several years been farmed in this country for their mozzarella-making milk, and reduced fat meat, but a few sites, such as The Wildlife Trust of South and West Wales' River Teifi, are now using them as part of their habitat management.

The buffalo are phenomenal grazers, and the reserve benefited not only from their reduction of invasive plants, but the shallow dragonfly pools and wader scrapes that resulted from their wallowing. They make a remarkable sight as you come round the corner, too.

LEARNING FROM NATURE

American footballers and motorbikers may one day owe their lives to woodpeckers, as the bird's extraordinary skull design is being studied to help enhance the resistance to impact of crash helmets. The woodpecker drums its beak against the bark of a tree at about 15 beats per second for a variety of reasons: alerting other woodpeckers to its territory, driving into the bark for beetles, and opening up a nest cavity in the trunk itself. If you or I had a beak and tried these tricks, we'd break our puny necks, or give ourself brain damage at the very least.

But not the woodpecker. The bird is able to bypass the trauma thanks to a system of muscular support structures at the back of its neck, a brain cavity packed with spongy shock-absorbent bone, another cavity, also shock-absorbent, in which the tongue sits coiled up, and the ability to hammer at a completely straight angle, so that all these counter-balances align. This means that, with every single ram of their head, woodpeckers can withstand the equivalent of 250 times the gravitational force felt by astronauts as they sit in their launching rockets.

CRYPTIC CREATURES AND PUZZLING PLANTS

Which of these botannical words has not been spelt correctly?
delphinium
fuchsia
sepal
saxifrage
groundsel
Answer on page 153

QUOTE UNQUOTE

The song of canaries
Never varies,
And when they're moulting
They're pretty revolting.
OGDEN NASH, US humorist

SITES FOR SORE EYES

Hannah Hauxwell, who became something of a celebrity some years ago once television discovered her solitary farming life, worked her land using traditional methods only, shunning artificial fertilisers and re-seeding techniques. For over 50 years, she ran Low Birk Hat Farm in County Durham, and upon her retirement in 1988, the Durham Wildlife Trust bought the land.

Now known as Hannah's Meadow, the reserve has changed very little over the centuries. Few sites anywhere in the country are as species-rich: meadow fox tail, sweet vernal grass and crested dog's-tail mix with wild flowers such as ragged robin, marsh marigold, yellow rattle and globe-flower. The Trust continues to manage the reserve by traditional methods: sheep lamb in the spring in the hay meadows; once the haycrop is cut in late July, the grass is allowed to grow until September when it is grazed by cattle. The sheep return in November before the winter rest period, when the dry stone walls are maintained, until the cycle can begin anew.

SCIENCE – IT'S CHILD'S PLAY

What does it take to discover a new British species? Hours of patience? A phenomenal understanding of your field? A fine microscope? Plenty of luck? Well, in some cases, it requires no more than being a five-year-old and playing in your back garden in Surrey. In 1997, Alysia Menzies, being just such an age, and doing just such a thing, spotted a ladybird on a plant which looked interesting to her. Fortunately she didn't eat it, but called the attention of the grown-ups, one of whom happened to be the coleopterist Ian Menzies. Called *Henosepilachna argus*, this Mediterranean immigrant which has since spread to other counties 'is a highly distinctive ladybird, 6-8mm in length and covered with short pubescence. Except for 11 round elytral spots, as well as the eyes and abdomen, which are black, the entire beetle is of a bright amber colour.' Ian's words, not Alysia's.

Lamb tree
A plant that grows a lamb, attached
by the navel. The lamb lives its short
life by eating the plant that supports it.
The lamb itself is mighty fine eating.
While watching other animals, the
young naturalist may wish to chew
on its fish-like meat, and drink
its honeyed blood.
Score: 10 pts.

NATURE NOTES

To me the most amazing thing was the spectacle of the swifts. It was
late for them, near the end of August; they should now have been far
away on their flight to Africa; yet here they were, delaying on that
desolate east coast in wind and wet, more than a hundred of them. It
was strange to see so many at one spot, and I could only suppose that
they had congregated previous to migration at that place, and were
being kept back by the late breeders, who had not yet been wrought up
to the pont of abandoning their broods. They haunted a vast ruinous
old barn-like building... over this building they hung all day in a crowd,
rising high to come down again at a frantic speed, and at each descent
a few birds could be seen to enter the holes, while others rushed out to
join the throng, and then all rose and came down again and swept
round and round in a furious chase, shrieking as if mad. At all hours
they drew me to that spot, and standing there, marvelling at their stay-
ing power and the fury that possessed them, they appeared to me like
tormented beings, and were like those doomed wretches in the halls of
Eblis whose hearts were in a blaze of unquenchable fire, and who, every
one with hands pressed to his breast, went spinning round in an everlasting agonised dance. They were tormented and crazed by the two
most powerful instincts of birds pulling in opposite directions – the
parental instinct and the passion of migration which called them to the
south.

WH Hudson, *Afoot in England*

WHEN IS A GOOSE NOT A GOOSE?

For centuries, the barnacle goose was thought to be a fish. This was because the bird, which graces Europe in the winter, flies off to the Arctic to breed in the summer. As people had no idea where it went, and never saw either eggs or goslings, they assumed it must be the offspring of creatures often found near its watery habitat, ie barnacles. Believing the goose grew within large bivalves until mature, they reasoned it was a fish, thus allowing Catholics to eat it on Fridays. The belief existed in many areas until the 18th century: one species of barnacle is even named *Lepas anatifera* – 'goose-bringer' – a title bestowed by Linnaeus in 1767.

IRON MUSSELS

How do mussels stick to rocks, rope, keels of boats, and indeed anything else they want to hang on to? The glue that they use is based on a series of cross-linked protein molecules, but the bonding agent that solidifies it is iron. The charged iron atoms are collected by the mussels from sea water, enabling them to create a type of superglue.

Environmental scientists are excited about this discovery. The shipping industry has long used toxic paints to kill off creatures like barnacles and mussels that attach themselves to the undersides of ships and slow them down, but now there is a chance of inventing a more 'friendly' protection, repelling the animals, rather than killing them.

IS YOU IS OR IS YOU AIN'T MY BABY?

The cuckoo is well-known for its ability to lay an egg in another bird's nest, pull back, and watch the foster parent seemingly not notice as the adopted young pushes the other eggs and young out of the nest, continually yells for food, and grows larger than the adult that feeds it. Over 100 species in Europe have been recorded doing the cuckoo's job for it, the commonest five in Britain being the:
1. Reed warbler
2. Dunnock
3. Meadow pipit
4. Pied wagtail
5. Robin

QUOTE UNQUOTE

A hen is only an egg's way of making another egg.
SAMUEL BUTLER, writer

SITES FOR SORE EYES

About a third of the world's entire breeding population of Manx shearwater breed at Skomer, the 760-acre island off Martin's Haven in Wales, near Haverfordwest. Run by the Wildlife Trust of South and West Wales, Skomer is the place to stay overnight during June and July to hear these extraordinary birds raise the roof with their cacophonous, coughing, raucous calls. Shearwaters nest in burrows, which they wriggle into on feet that were barely made for walking, yet at sea they are completely at home, arcing above the waves on long outstretched wings for decade upon decade.

Skomer is not just home to shearwaters, however. Kittiwakes, razorbills, puffins and guillemots are also on board in good numbers. Grey seals are present all year, pupping in September, while a race of bank vole is endemic to the island. Bluebells, then red campion, thrift, sea campion and heather make the isle an ever-changing palette throughout the year. The not too distant Stokholm island offers similiar treats.

CRYPTIC CREATURES AND PUZZLING PLANTS

Take the first letter from a dog to leave a bird of prey.
Answer on page 153

NATURE NOTES

Let me evoke the hawkmoths, the jets of my boyhood! Colours would die a long death on June evenings. The lilac shrubs in full bloom before which I stood, net in hand, displayed clusters of a fluffy grey in the dusk – the ghost of purple. A moist young moon hung above the mist of a neighbouring meadow... And suddenly it would come, the low buzz passing from flower to flower, the vibrational halo around the stream-lined body of an olive and pink hummingbird [hawk-]moth poised in the air above the corolla into which it had dipped its long tongue. Its handsome black larva (resembling a diminutive cobra when it puffed out its ocellated front segments) could be found on dank willow herb two months later. Thus every hour and season had its delights. And, finally, on cold, or even frosty, autumn nights, one could sugar for months by painting tree trunks with a mixture of molasses, beer, and rum. Through the gusty blackness, one's lantern would illumine the stickily glistening furrows of the bark and two or three large moths upon it imbibing the sweets, their nervous wings half open butterfly fashion, the lower ones exhibiting their incredible crimson silk from beneath the lichen-grey primaries. '*Catocala adultera!*' I would triumphantly shriek in the direction of the lighted windows of the house as I stumbled home to show my captures to my father.

Vladimir Nabokov, *Speak, Memory: an Autobiography Revisited*

---

122 *Number of individual trees left of the species* Serianthes nelsonii.
   121 live on Rota, the other one can be found on Guam

INTERNATIONAL DESTINATIONS
WITH A WILDLIFE TWIST

Head-Smashed-In Buffalo Jump, Canada
For 6,000 years the people of the North American plains killed bison by driving them over a precipice. This site is named after a young 19th century brave who climbed into a hollow in the cliff for a good view of the buffalo as they came over the top. He got a little closer than he should.

Elephantine Island, Egypt
Not any elephants to be seen, but the island probably gets its name from the mighty rocks in the river that surrounds it. It's likely that the isle was also once an ivory trading centre.

Chihuahua, Mexico
The ancient Aztecs kept this breed of dog as pets; their remains have been found in human graves. Chihuahua means 'dry sandy place' but today the state is Mexico's main producer of apples, walnuts, oats, cotton and jalapeno peppers. Historically, the city is significant for its role in the Mexican revolution of 1910; rebel leader Pancho Villa's former HQ is there, now a museum.

Kangaroo Island, South Australia
Australia's third largest island, close to Adelaide. In addition to kangaroos, it hosts wallabies, possums, bandicoots, koalas and the shy echidna and platypus. Off the coast is Seal Bay, home to around 600 sea lions, and from which dolphins and even whales can be seen. And there are little penguins and pelicans among the island's 240 bird species.

Pelican, Alaska
A small fishing town on the Lisianski Inlet on Chichagof Island, founded in 1938 by a fisherman who named it after his boat. Salmon fishing is particularly big here, so the main street is called Salmon Way. Most of the town is built on wooden pilings over tidal flats.

Bay of Pigs, Cuba
Famous for the failed 1961 US attempt to overthrow President Castro, the bay is today a haven for scuba divers and birdwatchers. The Las Salinas Wildlife Refuge has huge numbers of migrating birds including up to 10,000 pink flamingos. The memory of the invasion still dominates, however: yachts are still not allowed in the bay.

And closer to home...
Lizard Point, Cornwall
Mainland Britain's most southerly point, at the end of the Lizard peninsula. The word comes from the Cornish *lezou*, meaning headland. Marconi sent the first transatlantic radio signals from here in 1901 and the Goonhilly Satellite Earth Station is based here. Its huge white dishes receive and transmit pictures across two thirds of the world. There's also a seal sanctuary at Gweek.

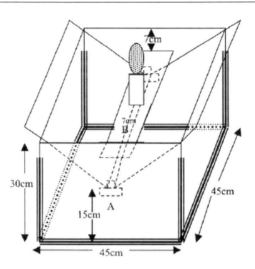

One of the best ways of finding out which moths inhabit your garden is to use a moth trap. As long as you release the moths the following morning, and keep them away from predators, this is a humane and accepted way of studying them.

Above is an outline plan of a Skinner trap. It is basically a 45cm square box with a bottom, 30cm high and made from 4mm plywood. The 'lid' is formed from two sloping sheets of 2mm Perspex with a 25mm gap between them at the bottom. The function of these Perspex sheets is to arrest the flight of the moth, funnelling it down into the trap.

The MV lamp must be operated with a ballast, which moderates the power when it is first switched on, allowing the bulb to warm up gradually; the ballast must be of the same wattage rating as the bulb. The bulb holder should be earthenware.

Finally, four or five egg trays, cut in half, need to be laid in the bottom of the trap for moths to sit in and under.

Of course, if you can't be bothered with all this palaver, moth traps are available without the fuss and bother. Try Anglian Lepidopterist Supplies (01263 862068) for good prices and excellent advice.

Chaos theory has it that if a butterfly flaps its wings in Tokyo there could be an earthquake in California. But how about if it flaps its wings in America, then magically appears four days later in Cornwall – what does chaos theory have to say about that?

The monarch butterfly, one of nature's most astonishing migrants, spends much of life pootling up or down the continent of America, yet occasionally the odd one or two turn up in Britain, the first sighting being in 1876. For years, it was assumed they had stowed away on board ships – after all, the monarch may be a mighty flyer, but the Atlantic is a far mightier ocean.

Yet in 1968 and 1981, the south-west coast of Britain was visited by monarchs in their dozens, at exactly the same time that several species of American birds, true rarities in this country, also turned up. Could the weather be playing a part? Then in 1995, on one day alone in October, at least 45 individual monarchs were spotted. Unusually, at the end of September that year, three hurricanes had hit the eastern seaboard of the US, resulting in a strong westerly airflow that culminated in a gale in south-western Britain on September 30. The air flow was reasonably warm, and travelled at around 30-35 knots, taking four days to cross the Atlantic, a short enough time for the butterflies to survive on their fat reserves. It was shown, conclusively, that it was possible for a butterfly to cross the Atlantic aided by nothing but the weather.

QUOTE UNQUOTE

Early to rise, early to bed, makes a chipmunk healthy, wealthy and dead.
JAMES THURBER, humorist

LAZY, HAZY DAYS OF SUMMER

We're all familiar with the concept of hibernation, the act of sleeping through the cold months to conserve energy. Yet some animals practise estivation, a state of torpor brought on during particularly hot and dry months. Snails are among the creatures that estivate. Once the air loses its humidity, some species start looking for a suitable hiding period during which to hide from the seasonal dryness, digging holes into the ground before winding down their systems. Other species, however, move upwards, climbing to the tops of plant stems, secreting mucus which dries and sticks them to the plant, while closing their shell aperture too.

A TOAD BY ANY OTHER NAME

Country names for the common toad

Bulgranack
Gangril
Hornywink
Jack
Josey
Puddock
Slug
Tod
Winky

ANIMAL CRACKERS

Japanese TV game shows are well-known the world over for encouraging their contestants to do bizarre things with animals – eating them, letting them crawl over them, being bitten by them. Yet the stupidity crown must now surely be passed to Chilean TV, which came up with the magnificent idea of the ultimate challenge. To win a car, all 30-year-old Maria Eugenia Berrios had to do was stay in a circus cage with two lions and two tigers for three minutes. It could work. But to spice it up, she had to pat one of them on the head.

Accepting the challenge, Maria entered the cage, gingerly approached one of the tigers, and gave it a pat. Minutes later, while being rushed to hospital with serious head and leg injuries, she must have wondered how badly she'd really wanted that car. Interestingly, Chilean TV management was furious with the game show producers for their 'irresponsibility'. Stronger words come to mind.

IDENTITY CRISIS

People who might be surprised to find that they're actually creatures or plants:

Cherry Laurel is a shrub
Douglas Fir is a tree
Herb Robert is a flower
Holly Blue is a butterfly
Jack Snipe is a bird
John Dory is a fish
Matt Knight is a fungus
Rose Chafer is a beetle
Phil Tufnell is a rabbit

126 Years, on publication of this book, that zander (or pike-perch) have been
living in Britain

MEANWHILE, IN A FOREIGN LAND...

In 1909, US President Teddy Roosevelt set off with an entourage of friends on one of the most destructive hunting safaris of all time. Starting in Mombasa, Kenya, they spent eight months blasting their way to Khartoum in Sudan. By the time they arrived, they had wiped out 5,013 mammals, 4,453 birds, 2,322 reptiles and amphibians, plus taken a huge and uncounted number of fish, insects, shells, and plants. The remains were sent to the Smithsonian Institute, where it was found that two subspecies were among the number: Teddy had succeeded in shoving a little further towards extinction both the Roosevelt's gazelle and the Roosevelt's sable. The sable, in particular, that was named after him is now one of Africa's most endangered antelope races. Talk about shooting yourself in the foot.

THE LIZARD'S DE-TAILS

Lizards have the ability to shed their tails for protection in a process known as 'autotomy'. The tail bones have a special weak spot at which a contraction of the muscles causes the bone to break and the tail to become loose. The separated tail continues to wriggle for several minutes, holding the attention of the predator, and the tailless lizard can make its escape.
After some months, the lizard grows a new tail, usually stumpier than the original and less flexible. Slow worms are also capable of autotomy, but are rarely able to grow a new tail afterwards.

WOULD YOU LIKE CRAB WITH YOUR MUSSELS?

We're all used to the possibility of finding insects in our food, but few expect to find a crab lurking there. The pea crab, which has a shell under a centimetre in diameter, makes its life in bivalves, such as mussels and clams, up and down the coast. One survey of the Western Solent found that 54% of the mussels collected had pea crabs living in them. The little crab, also known as a 'pinnothere', enjoys what, to humans, is an unappetising relationship with its hosts. It lays its eggs inside the bivalves, and feeds on the mussel's mucus from around its gills. It's likely that the mussel, meanwhile, eats the crab's faeces, as they're probably swept into its gills. When the crab isn't living inside mussels, it isn't averse to a meal of faeces, either, following periwinkles around for the deposited titbits they leave behind.

NATURE NOTES

Our ancestors, most of whom lived all the year round in unadulterated rural surroundings, took less conscious note of natural beauty, because it was the common air they breathed, the element in which they lived and moved. It pervaded and formed their minds and personalities. The Cavaliers drew their charm from the fields and the Roundheads their strength from the earth. Cavalier and Roundhead are alike a vanished race, for they are not to be bred under the influences of modern city life, machinery and the cheap press of today. So, too, it was the influence of the fields and woods of Elizabethan England that fostered the thousand-and-one lyric poets and musicians, those 'bards who died content on pleasant sward, leaving great verse unto a little clan'.

GM Trevelyan, *An Autobiography and Other Essays*

A WORLD IN MICROCOSM

There are more organisms in a spadeful of soil
than there are humans on the planet.

FROGS ARE FUNNY

A man walks into a bar, buys a pint, then says to the barman: 'Look at this'. He pulls a frog out of his pocket, and a tiny piano. The frog settles down at the piano, and bangs out a perfect performance of Rachmaninov's 3rd. The barman is amazed, but the man reaches into his other pocket.
'That's nothing,' he says, pulling out another frog, which he puts next to the first. This new frog breaks into a gorgeous rendition of *O Sole Mio*, accompanied immaculately by the pianist frog.
Another man comes up. 'Tell you what,' he says, 'I'll put money behind this bar to keep you in drink for the rest of the night, if you'll give me that singing frog.' The first man shrugs and agrees, and hands it over. As the new owner leaves, the barman says: 'Are you mad, you could have made a fortune with that singing frog.'
'Not really', says the man. 'The pianist is a ventriloquist.'

BEAUTY IS TRUTH

A Bambara poem in praise of the crowned crane, to some the most beautiful of birds. The crowned crane is the national symbol of Uganda.
The beginning of beginning rhythm
Is speech of the crowned crane.
The crowned crane says 'I speak'.
The word is beauty.

COUNTDOWN

In 2000, a few years before he died, the great ornithologist Chris Mead published *The State of the Nation's Birds*, which gave a full account of the status of our various species. The book revealed that Britain had a breeding population of:

7.1 million pairs of wren
4.2 million pairs of robin
2.35 million pairs of woodpigeon
1.05 million pairs of guillemot
240,000 pairs of moorhen
201,000 pairs of gannet
160,000 pairs of herring gull
126,300 pairs of lapwing

115,000 pairs of mallard
10,000 pairs of heron
50,000 pairs of kestrel
8,000 pairs of great crested grebe
300 pairs of red kite
131 pairs of marsh harrier
99 pairs of osprey
11 pairs of white-tailed eagle

QUOTE UNQUOTE

His imagination resembled the wings of an ostrich.
It enabled him to run, though not to soar.
BARON MACAULEY, on poet John Dryden

TRACKING WITH A DIFFERENCE

Many aerospace radar and weapon systems are given the names of plants or animals, including:

Blue Kestrel ....Radar of the Merlin ASW helicopter
Blue Tit..Early name for Sea Spray radar
Green Willow ....AI radar for single seat fighters
Mamba ....Mortar location radar
Orange Poodle...Low altitude radar system
Panther...Plessey GF75 surveillance radar
Possum..Low altitude air defence radar
Red Robin....................................CW radar for RAF Thunderbird II
Scorpion............................Blue Anchor TIR for export Bloodhound
Sea Owl.. GEC Marconi thermal imager
Winkle.. Passive tracking system
Yellow Tiger..Fire control radar

CRYPTIC CREATURES AND PUZZLING PLANTS

How many birds are sent by my true love on the
12th Day of Christmas?
Answer on page 153

NEW BALLS PLEASE

What happens to the 36,000 or more tennis balls used at the annual Wimbledon championships? Some of them get turned into homes. These new homes have small holes bored into them, and are attached to poles between 75cm and 1.5m off the ground. With luck, they will become inhabited by harvest mice, who can live there in comparative safety from birds of prey and weasels, which are too big to get through the hole. Harvest mice, which only weigh as much as a 20p piece, more traditionally weave their homes out of shredded grass and reeds part of the way up tall stalks. Yet intensive farming methods have brought their habitat, and in some areas their existence, under threat.

TALK LIKE AN EGYPTIAN

Egyptian hieroglyphics were symbols to represent objects or people, as well as sounds used for pronunciation. Here are some vocal sounds as represented by animals:

A, E, O

M

G, J

O, U, W

L, K

F, V

QUOTE UNQUOTE

I suffer from acute and incurable melophilia, *a rare and delightful ailment from which I am thankful that I can never be healed. The only symptom is a deep affection for badgers.*
PHIL DRABBLE, naturalist

SITES FOR SORE EYES

The cliffs of South Gower near Port Eynon in Wales is one of the great coastal havens of Britain. A mixture of habitats merge here, from limestone grassland and scree to maritime heath, rocky foreshore and caves to relict sand dune grassland. It's the only site anywhere in Britain where yellow whitlow grass grows, while the silky wave moth is one of its flagship species. Sea-watching can barely be matched, here, either, with rare birds recorded every year, while raven, chough and dartford warbler feature inland.

It's an impressive feeling to stand high on the cliffs knowing that ancient life once inhabited the rocks below. A medieval dovecote was built into the cliffs in more recent times, but the caves, which were inhabited 30,000 years ago, are some of the richest Upper Paleolithic prehistoric sites in Britain.

SOMETHING TO CROW ABOUT?

In November 2000, the *Countryside and Rights of Way Act* (CRoW) gained royal assent. This was the first major step forward in countryside protection since the *Wildlife and Countryside Act 1981*. It can be broken down into five main parts:

1. Deals with the 'right to roam'.

2. Clarifies uncertainties concerning rights of way.

3. The major wildlife section, covering Sites of Special Scientific Interest (SSSIs), enforcement of the laws pertaining to offences against wildlife, and the importance of biodiversity.

4. Requires management plans for Areas of Outstanding Natural Beauty (AONBs).

5. Various details, including local-access issues, countryside management agreements, and the registration of village greens.

Cowslips were once as common as buttercups, as the extract below from *Sons and Lovers* shows. Indeed, they were often used to make one of the countryside's most potent wines. Yet scenes such as that written about by Lawrence are now rare, and recipes such as that printed below are now frowned upon. The charity Plantlife now runs regular cowslip counts, in an attempt to understand the ecology of this flower once common across the country, but now restricted to suitable fields, and with a contracting range.

They found at the top of the hill a hidden wild field, two sides of which were backed by the wood, the other sides by high loose hedge of hawthorn and elder-bushes. Between these overgrown bushes were gaps that the cattle might have walked through had there been any cattle now. There the turf was smooth as velveteen, padded and holed by the rabbits. The field itself was coarse, and crowded with tall, big cowslips that had never been cut. Clusters of strong flowers rose everywhere above the coarse tussocks of bent. It was like a roadstead crowded with tall, fairy shipping.

DH Lawrence, *Sons and Lovers*, 1913

Cowslip wine
4 quarts freshly-picked cowslip flowers,
free from stalks and bits of green
4 quarts boiling water
3lbs loaf sugar
1 lemon
1 juicy orange
2 tablespoonfuls yeast
A little brandy, if liked

Pare the rinds very thinly from the orange and lemon, halve the fruit and press out the juice. Put this with the rinds into a tub or pan, and pour on the boiling water in which the sugar has been simmered for 30 minutes. (Any scum rising to the top while simmering should be carefully skimmed off.) When the liquid is lukewarm, stir in the flowers and yeast, and leave the tub covered with a cloth or flannel for three days, stirring twice a day. Then strain the liquid off, and pour it nearly all into a cask, leaving the bung loose till all working has stopped. Fill up with liquor kept over for the purpose, and bung up close. Leave undisturbed for three months before using. A little brandy will greatly improve it, but it is not necessary.

Farmhouse Fare, a collection of recipes from readers of
Farmers Weekly, first published 1948

GARDEN OF ENGLAND OR GARDEN OF EDEN?

Hybridisation between plants is not particularly uncommon, but every now and then one turns up that catches the eye more so than most. In June 1998, a hybrid orchid was discovered, new to Britain, called *xOrchiaceras melsheimeri*. Discovered in a Kent woodland, the plant is tall with a cylindrical spike and intermediate flowers. The hoods are crimson, and have tufts of red hairs, while the spur is very small, only about 1mm long.

What makes this hybrid so memorable? It was found within a mixed population of its parent plants... the man orchid and the lady orchid. Genesis begins anew.

HANDY PLANT NAMES TO KNOW WHEN YOU'RE IN THE MOOD FOR CUSSIN'

Bloody crane's-bill
Bastard toadflax
Devil's bit scabious
Fiddle dock
Frogbit
Hoary cress
Nipplewort
Pignut
Spotted medick
Stinking iris

YOU'RE SURE OF A BIG SURPRISE

When a home-owner in Henley-on-Thames called in the police to investigate a break-in in 2002, she was worried that her basement might have been burgled. Nothing seemed to have been stolen however, and the DNA testing on some blood found by the broken window revealed that if anything had been stolen, it couldn't have been anything larger than could fit in a wallaby's pouch. It seemed that the animal must have fallen into her basement area, broken the window, pulled itself together, and with one bound was free.

Wallabies are probably the most unusual of wild British animals. Escapes from parks and collections, generally in the south or the Midlands, they are not particularly successful, but the occasional colony survives for a while. In 1993, the estimated feral population in Britain was just 30, although this may have fallen in more recent years.

Wingspan, in millimetres, of the death's-head hawkmoth, 133
Britain's largest moth

NATURE NOTES

At times Noah was nearly on the edge. The Ark was behind schedule, the craftsmen had to be whipped, hundreds of terrified animals were bivouacking near his palace, and nobody knew when the rains were coming. God wouldn't even give him a date for that. Every morning we looked at the clouds: would it be a westerly wind that brought the rain as usual, or would God send his special downpour from a rare direction? And as the weather slowly thickened, the possibilities of revolt grew. Some of the rejected wanted to commandeer the Ark and save themselves, others wanted to destroy it altogether. Animals of a speculative bent began to propound rival selection principles, based on beast size or utility rather than mere number; but Noah loftily refused to negotiate. He was man who had his little theories, and he didn't want anyone else's.

Julian Barnes, *A History of the World in 10 1/2 Chapters*

WATER SPREAD

Canadian waterweed is the best known example of an alien aquatic plant 'rooting' itself in Britain, but it is not alone, as this list of introduced species with their first recorded dates shows:

Sweet-flag	1668
Canadian waterweed	1842
Bog arum	1861
Tapegrass	1868
Grass-leaved naiad	1883
Water fern	1886
Cape-pondweed	1906
Canadian arrowhead	1908
Duck-potato	1941
Various-leaved water-milfoil	1941
Curly waterweed	1944
Red water-milfoil	1944
South American waterweed	1948
Large-flowered waterweed	1953
New Zealand pigmyweed	1956
Parrot's-feather	1960
Narrow-leaved arrowhead	1962
Spatter-dock	1963
Nuttall's waterweed	1966
Fanwort	1969
Least duckweed	1977
Floating pennywort	1990
Slender sweet-flag	1986

QUOTE UNQUOTE

*The sun, with all those planets revolving around it and
dependent on it, can still ripen a bunch of grapes as if it had
nothing else in the universe to do.*
GALILEO GALILEI, astronomer

YOU'RE SURE OF A BIG SURPRISE

If you thought the only sizeable item on Salisbury Plain was
Stonehenge, then it may be time to rethink. In November 2003
permission was given to reintroduce the great bustard to the area, a bird
that was hunted to extinction in Britain in the 19th century. Forty
chicks are being introduced to the area each year from abandoned nests
in Russia for 10 years from June 2004, which if all goes well will grow
into huge whiskered turkey-like birds, each the size of an adult roe deer.

A similar programme at Porton Down was tried but failed in the 70s,
yet hopes are high that the Salisbury Plain experiment will work,
particularly in Wiltshire itself, for the bird adorns the county's coat of
arms. The Porton Down birds were bred in captivity, but by releasing
these new birds straight into the wild, it is believed that they will be
better able to fend for themselves.

OH NO! IT'S THEM!

There are about 50 different species of ant in Britain, many of which are impossible to tell apart without the aid of a good microscope. But the ants themselves know the differences, and in some cases, exploit them. The magnificently titled blood-red slave-making ant is not a species you want living near you if you're, say, a wood ant, for the slave-makers live up to their name.

In around July or August, they make their raids. A party of workers sets out early in the morning until they find the nest of another species which they then encircle. Once their numbers are high enough, they enter the nest and grab as many of the pupae inside that they can find. It's a desperate affair. Workers from the invaded nest are killed if they attack, while the other ants try to break through the invading lines with their pupae, or carry them away by climbing up vegetation. They are rarely successful.

Returning to their own nest with the pupae clamped in their jaws, the slave-makers have finished their job. The pupae will hatch and become workers themselves in their new colony.

MEANWHILE, IN A FOREIGN LAND

An 80-year-old elephant in Thailand was given a new lease of life in 2003. Unable to chew her food, Morakot had become so weak that even injected saline solution, vitamins and antibiotics seemed unlikely to save her life. So another solutions was found: dentures. They were made from stainless steel, silicone and plastic, and measured six inches in width and length.

Elephants normally grow four sets of teeth during a lifetime, but once they've lost their last molar they cannot chew properly and often die from malnutrition or starvation. Unless, of course, there's a handy elephant dentist nearby.

CRYPTIC CREATURES AND PUZZLING PLANTS

Which of the following is not a moth?
Transparent burnet
Great burnet
Five-spot burnet
Six-spot burnet
New Forest burnet
Answer on page 153

NATURE NOTES

Then they all went together into the woods, looking everywhere among bushes and brambles to see if they could find the head. And, wonder of wonders, God in his wisdom sent a wolf to watch over the head, and protect it against other wild beasts day and night. The men went about searching, and constantly calling out to one another, as is the custom of woodsmen, 'Where art thou now, my companion?' And the head answered them, saying, 'Here, here, here'. Every time they called the head spoke back to them. There lay the grey wolf watching over the head, with it clasped between his two forepaws. He was greedy and hungry, yet for the sake of God he dared not eat the head but preserved it from other creatures. Then were the men amazed at the wolf's guardianship, and took the holy head away with them, thanking the Almighty for the miracle. And the wolf followed them as they bore away the head, until they came to the town, just as if he were tame, and then returned to the forest.

**From a 10th century description of Saxons hunting for the head
of their murdered King Edmund**

WHAT YOU GET AS A MEMBER OF
THE WILDLIFE TRUSTS

• *Natural World* magazine three times a year. This award-winning colour magazine is full of compelling articles, stunning photography and the latest wildlife news.

• A newsletter or magazine from your local Wildlife Trust, keeping you informed about the wildlife on your doorstep.

• Details of the Wildlife Trust nature reserves in your area.

• Invitations to local events, many of them free.

• Opportunities to lend a hand and play a direct role in helping local wildlife.

• The knowledge that you have helped keep the UK's precious wildlife safe for the future.

• For further information visit www.wildlifetrusts.org.

RESEARCH ALL WASHED UP

Researchers from Bristol University in 2001 were amazed to find that bats that they were monitoring with radio transmitters had all taken to the water. Bats often fly low over water, taking insects with their feet, and should they accidentally find themselves in the water, can get out... but this was different. The signals received from the transmitters showed one bat slowly moving into a pool of water, gradually joined by the others, until they had crossed to the other side. The researchers were dumbfounded and excited. Was this new behaviour being exhibited?

Meanwhile, another group of researchers from Oxford University had been monitoring voles. They too reported in some extraordinary mammalian behaviour. Also using radio transmitters, they observed the voles launch themselves into the air... and stay there, reaching speeds of up to six miles per hour as they twisted and turned in the night sky. *Voler* may be French for 'to fly', but this was ridiculous.

Some time later, the two groups happened to meet up. Each told the other of their fascinating findings. Each mentioned the night they'd been researching: it was the same one. Each revealed the stretch of water they'd been monitoring: it was the same one.

Each began slowly to realise that they'd been using identical radio frequencies, and monitoring each other's animals.

MEANWHILE, IN A FOREIGN LAND...

Many creatures give off an alarm call as a predator approaches, but it can be important for the other members of their group to know which kind of predator it is they should be fleeing, as the vervet monkey of Africa has worked out.

When a vervet monkey sentry sees a leopard it gives a loud bark, the signal to other vervets to leap into the trees where the leopard can't reach.

Yet what if the the predator is an eagle? The treetops are the worst place to be, so the sentry emits a coughing call, the sign to dash to the ground and hide in a bush.

If the predator is a snake, however, then a bush may be a foolish place to hide. A third, sharper call alerts the other vervets to stand on their hind legs to spot the snake for themselves and keep their distance.

QUOTE UNQUOTE

No animal ever invented anything as bad as drunkenness – or so good as drink.
GK CHESTERTON, author

NATURE NOTES

Leaving my fishing tackle and a few small fish under the apple tree to be called for on my way home, I climbed over the hedge and was in Gedges Wood, which quite easily became something else. In the sun-flecked shade under the leafy chestnut poles there was a smell of wild garlic; and there were cushions of moss between the roots of oak trees where I could sit and listen; or I could clamber into the upper branches and be a look-out man in the full glory of the happy late afternoon sunshine. Or I would go on until I arrived at the banks of a small stream which lost itself in some marshy ground at the foot of the hill. This was a rushy region where there was a moorhen's nest among the sedges, and there was a jungle path through it where the thistles and ragwort grew higher than my head. It was a famous place for moths and butterflies. There were Cinnabar moths and lazy marsh-ringlets and three kinds of skippers (Dingy, Chequered and Grizzled). I once told my mother that I'd seen a Purple Emperor there, and her sympathetic enthusiasm almost made me believe that I had; and anyhow it was the sort of place where I ought to have seen one.

Siegfried Sassoon, *The Old Century*

FROGS ARE FUNNY

A man goes into a cinema with his frog to watch a film. There's a funny scene early on, and the frog starts laughing. A little later on the mood turns sadder and suddenly the frog starts crying.
This goes on throughout the entire film, the frog laughing and crying at all the right places. A woman nearby has been watching the whole thing and on the way out goes up to the man and says, 'That's truly amazing!'
'It certainly is,' he replies. 'He hated the book!'

TALKING NATURALLY

Bald as a coot
Their white head patches give coots an appearance of baldness.

As happy as a clam at high tide
At high tide, clams are free from the attentions of their predators.

The bee's knees
Bees carry pollen back to the hive in sacs on their legs. The allusion is to the concentrated goodness to be found around the bee's knee.

Crocodile tears
Crocodiles have glands that secrete liquid to keep their eyelids moist when out of the water. These glands are sometimes stimulated when the crocodile is eating.

Pop goes the weasel
To pop is to pawn something, and a weasel and stoat is a coat. Thus, once you've been in and out of the eagle (a pub), you've run out of money and have to pawn your clothes. Well, that's the way the money goes.

Raining cats and dogs
The phrase is supposed to have originated in the 17th century. City streets were filthy and heavy rain would occasionally carry along dead animals. Richard Brome's *The City Witt*, 1652, includes the line: 'It shall rain dogs and polecats'.

Weasel words
Words that suck the life out of the words next to them, just as a weasel sucks the egg and leaves the shell.

White elephant
White, or albino, elephants were regarded as holy in ancient Thailand: to keep one was a very expensive task. Thus, a gift of a white elephant was an unwanted thing, for it would ruin you.

Make the beast with two backs
An older phrase than might be assumed. In *Othello*, Iago explains: 'I am one, sir, that comes to tell you your daughter and the Moor are now making the beast with two backs'.

ORDER, ORDER

My house is full of animals
I don't know what to do
I think I'm going crazy –
I'm living in a zoo!
Song by Darrell Bowen and Dave Holmes

On 29 March 2000, David Amess MP stood up in the House of Commons and said: 'A few weeks ago, a scurrilous article appeared that claimed that the House of Commons was full of animals. It said that the Conservative benches are full of dinosaurs, the Labour benches full of sheep and the Liberal benches full of dead parrots. As we all know, that clearly is not the case. The only animals in the House of which I am aware are the delightful guide-dog of the [then] Secretary of State for Education and Employment, the springer spaniels that sniff round the place before our proceedings start and the mouse or rat that decided to make an appearance on the floor of the Chamber a few weeks ago.'

He was begging to move that leave be given to bring in a bill to amend the *Zoo Licensing Act 1981* so as to make it unlawful to operate a circus except with the authority of a licence.

CRYPTIC CREATURES AND PUZZLING PLANTS

My goodness, what connects the following:
Ostrich; toucan; kangaroo; bear; seal; pelican; tortoise; lion; kinkajou?
Answer on page 153

SITES FOR SORE EYES

Rutland Water, run by the Leicestershire and Rutland Wildlife Trust, has probably become best known today for its annual hosting of the British Birdwatching Fair, an event that draws thousands of visitors, and raises dozens of thousands of pounds for international conservation. Yet the reserve itself should not be ignored: it's one of the best inland sites for passage waders, and up to 23,000 birds have been recorded within its boundaries on a single day.

In addition to the Bewick's swans and little ringed plovers, gadwall and shoveler, the site hosts a wide variety of wild flowers such as ragged robin and cuckooflower, as well as 24 species of butterfly and dragonfly.

STRANGELY OMITTED FROM THE
I-SPY BOOK OF ANIMALS

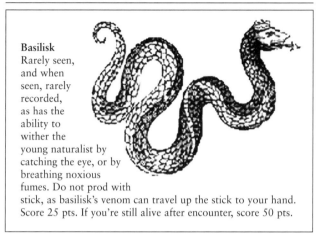

Basilisk
Rarely seen, and when seen, rarely recorded, as has the ability to wither the young naturalist by catching the eye, or by breathing noxious fumes. Do not prod with stick, as basilisk's venom can travel up the stick to your hand. Score 25 pts. If you're still alive after encounter, score 50 pts.

POTTERING AROUND THE CEMETERY

Beatrix Potter, whose books have been stored in the childhood nostalgia banks of a century's worth of readers, created a range of countryside characters whose names are known to many. But where did those names come from: a fertile imagination?

The answer appears to be a little more morbid. Potter was born in London at 2 Bolton Gardens, West Brompton, just up the road from Brompton Cemetery, where she probably often took youthful strolls. Many of the headstones have disappeared over the years, swallowed up by lengthening grasses, the names they bore worn away by the decades. Yet recent research has revealed that some of the inhabitants of the cemetery bore a surprising resemblance to Potter's characters.

William McGregor and Kelvin Brock alone could have been put down to coincidence – Farmer McGregor and Tommy Brock (from *The Tailor of Gloucester*) aren't particularly unusual names – but by the time you get to Noel Nutkins, (Squirrel Nutkin?), eyebrows are beginning to raise. Further down the list you come to Jeremiah Fisher (Jeremy Fisher?), and you know you're on to something. If only there was a clincher.

And there is. In addition to those above, Brompton graveyard was also the final resting place of one Peter Rabbett.

HIGHLIGHTS OF THE WILDLIFE AND COUNTRYSIDE ACT

In 1981 the government passed the strongest piece of legislation yet on wildlife protection in Great Britain. Several amendments and specific new laws have been passed since, but this act has still been the principal bedrock of British conservation for two decades.

It is divided into four parts: wildlife, the countryside and national parks, public rights of way, and miscellaneous extras. These are the highlights of part one, which is divided into 27 sections:

Sections 1-8: Protection of birds
Prohibits the intentional killing, injuring or taking of any wild bird (except game species and pests) and the taking, damaging or destroying of the nest or eggs. It prohibits possession of wild birds or their eggs. It goes on to give powers to the Secretary of State to designate areas of special protection to provide further protection to birds and even prohibit disturbance or restrict access. Use of certain types of trap, poison, birdlime, etc, for catching or injuring birds is prohibited, as are certain methods of killing. It also prohibits sale or other forms of trade of wild live birds, eggs, and certain dead birds, and draws up guidelines for possession of certain species, and standards for their captivity.

Sections 9-12: Protection of other animals
Prohibits the intentional killing, injuring, possession of and trade in wild animals. In addition, places used for animal shelter and protection are safeguarded against intentional damage, destruction and obstruction and certain animals may not intentionally be disturbed while occupying those places. The Act offers leniency under some circumstances, such as the nursing of animals, or humane destruction of injured animals, and provides cover for incidental actions that are an unavoidable result of an otherwise lawful activity. Certain types of weapons (bows, explosives, poisons and electrical devices) are also prohibited.

Section 13: Protection of plants
Prohibits the unauthorised intentional uprooting of any wild plant species and forbids any picking, uprooting or destruction of certain species. It also prohibits the sale, trade, or possession for the purpose of sale of these plants. Common law kicks in with some species: many wild plants may be picked for personal use, covering customs such as blackberry-picking, mushroom-hunting, plucking ivy and holly at Christmas, and gathering sloes. To exercise this right you must be somewhere you have a legal right to be – such as a public footpath or public park.

Sections 14-15: Miscellaneous
Prohibits the release to the wild of alien species. The remaining 12 sections of the Act refer to the legal mechanisms for enforcing and licensing these laws.

NATURE NOTES

Birds that hunt have to be hooded; Thea had this thing ready, a tufted cover with drawstrings that you struck or loosened before you released the animal to rise and wait on its game. But before the eagle would take the hood he had to be thoroughly mastered, and I carried him on my arm some four hours without sleep. He wouldn't drop off, and Thea kept me awake. This was in Nuevo Laredo, just over the border. We put up in a hotel full of flies, a brown room with giant coarse cactus almost in the window... The flies nipped me because I had only one hand free and anyhow didn't want to startle him...

There had been an amazing crowd when we drove up to the hotel and opened the back door of the station wagon. In a few minutes more than 50 men and children had gathered. The eagle cam on my hand for his meat and the kids screamed, 'Ay! Mira, mira – el aguila, el aguila!' Some sight, I guess, since I'm fairly tall and wore that height-increasing hat and whipcord breeches, and, moreover, obviously followed the lead of Thea's beauty and importance. And anyway the eagle has ancient respect in Mexico from the old religion and the great class of knights in those days of obsidian sword slaughter that Diaz del Castillo witnessed. The children, I said, were screaming, while he rocked on my fist, 'El aguila, el aguila!' And because I heard Spanish for the first time, it was another word I made out, the Roman name of Caligula. I thought in my heart how suitable it was. Caligula!

'El aguila!'

'Si, Caligula,' I said. That name was the first satisfaction I had in him.

Saul Bellow, *The Adventures of Augie March*

QUOTE UNQUOTE

When the eagles are silent, the parrots begin to jabber.
SIR WINSTON CHURCHILL, politician, on other politicians

THE BRITISH MONGOOSE?

Probably the only British mammal to make a habit of killing and eating adders is the hedgehog, which not only carries a certain immunity to the snake's venom, but also carries at least 6,000 other weapons – its spikes. By poking and prodding at the adder, slipping in little bites when it can, the hedgehog lures the snake into an attack, which it fends off with its spikes. Impaling or wounding itself on the sharp points, the snake steadily weakens, until it is incapable of further attacks or flight. Then the hedgehog pounces, and the battle is over.

HAVE A WHALE OF A TIME

Believe it or not, at least 25 species of cetacean – porpoise, dolphin and whale – have been seen in British waters, 11 of them on an annual basis. Here is a list of some of your best cetacean-watching areas:

Common or harbour porpoise
The only British porpoise, best seen off the north-west coast of Britain

Bottle-nosed dolphin
The most frequently seen dolphin, particularly as it tends to move in sociable groups. It breeds in the Moray Firth and Cardigan Bay

Common dolphin
Found along the west coast and in the North Sea

Striped dolphin
Rare; found to the south-west of Britain

Orca, or killer whale
Occasionally seen in northern areas of the North Sea and off the Atlantic coastline

Atlantic white-sided dolphin
North of Scotland

White-beaked dolphin
The west coast of Ireland and the northern North Sea

Risso's dolphin
The western areas of the English Channel to the north of Scotland

Fin whale
The second largest whale in the world can be seen from north Scotland to south-west Ireland

Minke whale
Most easily seen from land, particularly the Shetland Islands

Sperm whale
Dives for a long time, so difficult to spot, even off the west coasts of Scotland and Ireland

Long-finned pilot whale
Can be seen migrating late in the year in the northern seas in large pods

Cuvier's beaked whale
The deep waters of the North Atlantic

Northern bottle-nosed whale
The deep waters of the North Atlantic during summer

Several other species have also been occasionally recorded, including the northern right whale, humpbacked whale, and Beluga whale. Astonishingly, even the blue whale, earth's largest ever creature has been seen, albeit rarely.

DON'T COUNT YOUR FROGS BEFORE THEY'RE HATCHED

A frog's egg is a vulnerable thing to be. A spawning female lays around 2,000 of them, yet only about 2% of them, at best, survive into adulthood.

ANIMAL CRACKERS

Zoos around the world have been going through difficult times in recent years. Many have had to reshape their function, concentrating on education, conservation issues, and protection of endangered species to encourage people worried about seeing animals in captivity back through the turnstiles. Yet one zoo in Dandong, China, recently tried a rather novel approach to its marketing strategy. It handed out rifles at the gate and allowed its visitors to shoot the animals.

Protests naturally rang out, but the zoo defended itself by stating that the animals were being shot under controlled circumstances, it was only a bit of fun, and, anyway, folks weren't allowed to shoot the rare ones, good heavens no.

It seems that such a carefully constructed argument fell on deaf ears, and the zoo reverted to the old-fashioned approach of animal protection in 2003.

NATURE NOTES

I often pulled my hat over my eyes to watch the rising of the lark, or to see the hawk hang in the summer sky and the kite take its circles round the wood. I often lingered a minute on the woodland stile to hear the woodpigeons clapping their wings among the dark oaks. I hunted curious flowers in rapture and muttered thoughts in their praise. I loved the pasture with its rushes and thistles and sheep-tracks. I adored the wild, marshy fen with its solitary heronshaw sweeing along in its melancholy sky. I wandered the heath in raptures among the rabbit burrows and golden-blossomed furze. I dropt down on a thymy mole-hill or mossy eminence to survey the summer landscape... I marked the various colours in flat, spreading fields, checkered into closes of different-tinctured grain like the colours of a map; the copper-tinted clover in blossom; the sun-tanned green of the ripening hay; the lighter charlock and the sunset imitation of the scarlet headaches; the blue corn-bottles crowding their splendid colours in large sheets over the land and troubling the cornfields with destroying beauty; the different greens of the woodland trees, the dark oak, the paler ash, the mellow lime, the white poplars peeping above the rest like leafy steeples, the grey willow shining in the sun, as if the morning mist still lingered on its cool green... I observed all this with the same raptures as I have done since. But I knew nothing of poetry. It was felt and not uttered.

John Clare, *The Autobiography*

SITES FOR SORE EYES

Monkwood, near Worcestershire's Sinton Green, has a long and deserved reputation as a magnificent reserve for butterflies and moths. 36 species of the former have been seen here, along with over 500 species of moth. Wood white, white admiral and silver-washed fritillary are among the highlights, but look out too for dragonfly specialities such as the emperor.

If butterflies are in abundance, then the reserve must boast an impressive floral variety, and it does. Spring brings early purple orchids, lily-of-the-valley, ragged robin and ramsons. Knapweed, meadowsweet, melilot and betony are among the summer attractions, while autumn introduces an impressive display of fungi. The reserve is jointly owned by the Worcestershire Wildlife Trust and Butterfly Conservation.

A BUNCH OF DICKY BIRDS

Frog and toad – road
Apples and pears – stairs
Pig's ear – beer
Rabbit and pork – talk
Daisy roots – boots
Hearts of oak – broke
Flounder and dab – cab
Grasshopper – copper
Turtle dove – love
Haddock and bloater – motor (car)
Salmon and trout – pint of stout
Tom tit – Nobody knows what this is supposed to mean, but it may be some kind of faecal product

ANIMAL CRACKERS

Every year, the Hong Kong government-run radio station RTHK holds a Person of the Year contest. In 2003, the title was changed to Personality of the Year. This was because the winner was a crocodile.

Believed to be an escaped pet, the 1.5m croc ran loose on the Hong Kong-China border for months, evading capture by expert crocodile hunters. Put forward onto the poll as a joke, it won comfortably, pulling in 36% of the vote, and easily beating the collective Hong Kong hospital workers into second place.

Further down the list came Hong Kong's leader Tung Chee-hwa, who polled less than 5% of the vote.

Peat is an organic material that forms in the waterlogged, sterile, acidic conditions of bogs and fens. These conditions favour the growth of mosses, especially sphagnum. As plants die, they do not decompose. Instead, the organic matter is laid down, and slowly accumulates as peat because of the lack of oxygen in the bog.

A little over 3% of the earth's land surface is covered in peat, but not all peatlands are the same. Just as forests in Brazil, Canada and England are very different, so too are peatlands in Alaska, Indonesia and Europe, each supporting its own native plants and animals. Peat has the ability to preserve materials and this has led to some remarkable finds in peat bogs, including people buried thousands of years ago and wooden artefacts that have not survived elsewhere.

The importance of peatlands has been recognised by the European Union which has identified a number of bogs as priority habitats for conservation under the Habitats and Species Directive. Peat bogs contribute to the welfare of all living things by 'locking up' carbon that would otherwise increase the greenhouse effect. Carbon, removed from the atmosphere over thousands of years, is released when bogs are drained and peat starts to decompose.

Originally, lowland raised bog (the rarest type in the UK) covered nearly 95,000ha. Now only 6,000ha remain in a near natural state.

Agriculture and forestry have damaged large areas of peatland. But today, commercial peat extraction to supply gardeners and nursery growers is the major threat. Peat has been cut and used as a fuel for many centuries. Hand-cutting of peat is a slow, labour-intensive process that can allow the bog partially to recover. It is very different from industrialised, mechanical extraction practised by peat companies, which drain and damage whole bogs. The companies deep-drain peatlands and strip all vegetation from vast expanses of bog surface.

Peat bogs desperately need your help. You can help save them by:

• Refusing to buy peat or plants grown in peat. If your garden centre doesn't stock them, ask why not. Details of where to buy peat-free products are available from The Wildlife Trusts.

• Stop using peat in your garden; start a compost heap that will provide an alternative.

• Find out if your local authority has signed the peatland protection charter (details from your local Wildlife Trust).

• Visit a peatland reserve near to you and see its wildlife. Your local Wildlife Trust can help you. Once you have, you'll never want to buy peat again.

QUOTE UNQUOTE

To the dull mind nature is leaden; to the illumined mind the whole world burns and sparkles with light.
RALPH WALDO EMERSON, US poet and philosopher

NATURE NOTES

The wild creatures I had come to Africa to see are exhilarating in their multitudes and colours, and I imagined for a time that this glimpse of the earth's morning might account for the anticipation that I felt, the sense of origins, of innocence and mystery, like a marvellous childhood faculty restored. Perhaps it is the consciousness that here in Africa, south of the Sahara, our kind was born, But there was also something else that, years ago, under the sky of the Sudan, had made me restless, the stillness in this ancient continent, the echo of so much that has died away, the imminence of so much as yet unknown. Something has happened here, is happening, will happen – whole landscapes seem alert.
Peter Matthiessen, *The Tree where Man was Born*

READ ALL ABOUT IT

In 2003, the BBC ran a poll to discover the nation's favourite novels. In addition to books about creatures like *Winnie the Pooh* and *Black Beauty*, 14 of the top 100 books had plants or animals in their titles. The books, in their final positions, were:

6. *To Kill a Mockingbird,* Harper Lee
9. *The Lion, the Witch and the Wardrobe,* CS Lewis
13. *Birdsong,* Sebastian Faulks
15. *The Catcher in the Rye,* JD Salinger
16. *The Wind in the Willows,* Kenneth Grahame
29. *The Grapes of Wrath,* John Steinbeck
46. *Animal Farm,* George Orwell
50. *The Shell Seekers,* Rosamunde Pilcher
57. *Swallows and Amazons,* Arthur Ransome
59. *Artemis Fowl,* Eoin Colfer
64. *The Thorn Birds,* Colleen McCollough
66. *The Magic Faraway Tree,* Enid Blyton
70. *Lord of the Flies,* William Golding
92. *The Clan of the Cave Bear,* Jean M Auel

In addition, Stella Gibbons (*Cold Comfort Farm*) was among the writers.

SNAKES ALIVE!

Britain has six species of native reptile: adder, grass snake, smooth
snake, slow worm, common lizard and sand lizard.
What makes them reptiles?

1. Their bodies are covered with scales or horny plates.
2. They are cold blooded which means they control their body
temperature by getting their heat directly from the sun or other warm
objects, rather than from the food they eat.
3. Snakes and lizards have teeth which are continually replaced
throughout their life.
4. Reptiles also shed their skins at least once a year depending on
species, and you may find a discarded, colourless skin in summer
months. Shedding or 'sloughing' allows the reptile to grow, and helps
dispose of parasites, dirt and deposits on the skin.
5. The adder and the common lizard give birth to live young, but
other reptiles lay eggs.
6. Please note that Jeffrey Archer is in fact a mammal.

SHELLING OUT

The seven species of marine turtle around the world are

Australian flatback
Olive Ridley
Loggerhead
Kemp's Ridley
Green
Hawksbill
Leatherback

All but the first two have been recorded in British and Irish waters. The
earliest recorded sighting was in 1684 from Orkney. The first specific
identification was of a leatherback in 1756 off Cornwall. It ended up as
a centrepiece in a Penzance feast.

QUOTE UNQUOTE

*Everything is blooming most recklessly; if it were voices instead of
colors, there would be an unbelievable shrieking into the
heart of the night.*
RAINER MARIA RILKE, German poet

NATURE NOTES

The English countryside is rapidly becoming a managed one, in which the overwhelming dominance of efficient agriculture is no longer determining all change. Much of the rural scene is diversifying, but in the process we find ourselves increasingly thinking of management for recreation or 'wildlife'. Inside our gardens, once jealously secluded, a parallel change is taking place, and the pressure of manicured tidiness relaxes. To the European tourist much of rural England already looks like a garden. Is this what we want? Even if it is not, can we define and carry through any alternative policy? These are debatable questions for the 21st century.

Max Walters, *Wild and Garden Plants*

A NATION OF INSECTS

Below are the 27 orders of British insect. The numbers in brackets are the total British species, sometimes approximated. These numbers frequently change as new classification discoveries are made.

Diptera – Two-winged flies (6,670)
Hymenoptera – Bees, wasps, ants and allies (6,500)
Coleoptera – Beetles (4,000)
Lepidoptera – Butterflies and moths (2,500)
Hemiptera – True bugs (1,650)
Mallophaga – Biting lice (500)
Collembola – Springtails (300)
Trichoptera – Caddis-flies (190)
Thysanoptera – Thrips (150)
Psocoptera – Booklice (90)
Neuroptera – Lacewings (69)
Siphaptera – Fleas (60)
Anoplura – Sucking lice (50)
Ephemeroptera – Mayflies (47)
Odonata – Dragonflies and damselflies (40)
Plecoptera – Stoneflies (34)
Orghoptera – Grasshoppers and crickets (30)
Strepsiptera – Stylopids (20)
Diplura – Two-pronged bristletails (12)
Protura – Tiny wingless insects with no common name (12)
Thysanura – Bristletails (9)
Dictyoptera – Cockroaches (6)
Dermaptera – Earwigs (4)
Mecoptera – Scorpion-flies (4)
Phasmida – Stick insects (4 introduced species)
Raphidioptera – Snakeflies (4)
Megaloptera – Alderflies (3)

DURING THE COMPILATION OF THIS BOOK, THE COMPANION TEAM...

Watched 107.4 hours of nature TV programming

Came into work with bird droppings on their clothes three times

Bought a wildlife calendar in January and lost it in March

Visited 17 nature reserves

Tried to perfect their lion impressions but came off more like
a troupe of constipated baboons

Finally worked out the difference between pearl-bordered
and small pearl-bordered fritillary

Mentioned the word 'fossa' 453 times

Fed 209 pigeons in the park, probably illegally

Developed a new and unexpected interest in lichens

Found the calendar again in May

Started testing the comparative strengths of crab grips. Stopped after
the first one

Decided that frogs aren't particularly funny after all

*Please note that although every effort has been made to ensure
accuracy in this book, the above facts may be the result of wild and
woolly minds.*

When one tugs at a single thing in nature, he finds it attached to the rest of the world.

John Muir, naturalist

The answers. As if you needed them.

P14.   Beech

P19.   Nightingale

P29.   Eider

P34.   Flicker – it's an American woodpecker.

P43.   Linnet

P54.   Fox: Ox

P58.   Zorilla – it's a striped member of the weasel family that shoots noxious anal secretions at you if you get too close.

P67.   Rusty-spotted cat – it's the world's smallest species of cat, weighing just 1.5kg.

P75.
```
   |T|AME
M |I |LE
   |G|OLD
M |E |ND
   |R|IGHT
```

P83.   Hoverfly

P98.   Piddock – it's a seashore mollusc.

P110.
```
   |L|UST
N |E |T
   |M|IME
P |O |ACH
   |N|EAR
```

P115. Betony

P118. Botanical only has one 'n'.

P122. Beagle: Eagle

P129. 23

P136. Great burnet – it's a plant.

P140. They've all advertised Guinness.

Summer makes me drowsy.
Autumn makes me sing.
Winter's pretty lousy,
But I hate Spring.

Dorothy Parker, wit

ACKNOWLEDGEMENTS

We gratefully acknowledge permission to reprint extracts of copyright material in this book from the following authors, publishers and executors:

Extract from *In Pursuit of Spring* by Edward Thomas by kind permission of Myfanwy Thomas

Extract from *The Man Who Planted Trees* by Jean Giono published by The Harvill Press. Used by permission of The Random House Group Limited

Extract from *Common Ground* by Richard Mabey by kind permission of J M Dent Ltd, Orion Publishing Group. Copyright © Richard Mabey 1980

Extract from *Men and the Fields* by Adrian Bell by kind permission of the Estate of Adrian Bell

Extract from *The Enchanted Canopy* by Andrew Mitchell by kind permission of HarperCollins Publishers Ltd. © 1986 Andrew Mitchell

Extract from *Time Will Darken It* by William Maxwell published by The Harvill Press/Vintage. Used by permission of The Random House Group Limited

Extract from *A Countrywoman's Notes* by Rosemary Verey © 1989. Reproduced by permission of Frances Lincoln Limited, 4 Torriano Mews, Torriano Avenue, London NW5 2RZ

Extract from *Meetings with Remarkable Trees* by Thomas Pakenham by kind permission of W & N Illustrated

Extract from *A Year In The Life Of a Field* by Michael Allaby (© Michael Allaby 1981) by permission of PFD (www.pfd.co.uk) on behalf of Michael Allaby

Extract from *Wild and Garden Plants* by Max Walters by kind permission of HarperCollins Publishers Ltd. © 1990 Max Walters

Extract from *The New Naturalists* by Peter Marren by kind permission of HarperCollins Publishers Ltd. © 1995 Peter Marren

Extract from *The Worm Forgives the Plough* by John Stewart Collis by kind permission of A P Watt Ltd on behalf of Michael Holroyd

Extract from *A History of the World in 10 1/2 Chapters* by Julian Barnes by kind permission of Macmillan Books

INDEX

The Wildlife Trusts are the UK's leading wildlife conservation charity. Through our network of 47 Wildlife Trusts and our junior branch Wildlife Watch, we work to protect wildlife in all habitats across the UK in towns, the countryside, our coasts and seas. We have more than 560,000 members, 24,000 volunteers and 1,500 members of staff, all playing a vital and active role in our work. We also manage more than 2,500 nature reserves, some of the finest in the UK, from Scottish islands to tiny green gems in the heart of cities. We play a crucial role in the survival of many wildlife species including Manx shearwater, otter, osprey and the red squirrel.

Our award-winning visitor centres welcome thousands of people each year, and offer unbeatable proximity to wildlife, often in comfortable surroundings, with shops, cafes and other facilities.

Members of The Wildlife Trusts receive:

- a copy of *Natural World*, a full colour magazine full of the latest wildlife news and views

- a copy of their local Trust magazine, updating them on activities in their region

- details of hundreds of events and volunteering opportunities information on special offers to members

- and the knowledge that their support is crucial in keeping the UK's wildlife safe for the future.

For more information, contact The Wildlife Trusts, tel: 0870 0367711 or visit www.wildlifetrusts.org